Altared Boy

Altared Boy

LCdr David Lewis, MSM, CD (Ret'd)

Published by

Battle Rattle Press

Copyright © 2022 David Lewis

All rights reserved. No part of this publication may be reproduced, stored in a retrieval system or transmitted in any form or by any means – electronic, mechanical, photocopying, and recording or otherwise – without prior written permission from the author. The exception would be brief passages by a reviewer in a newspaper or magazine or online. To perform any of the above is an infringement of copyright law.

ISBN: 978-1-7781321-0-0

Published by Battle Rattle Press

WARNING:

Altared Boy deals with issues of clerical sexual abuse which some readers may find disturbing. If you find any of the content triggering, or need to talk to someone, confidential 24-hour support is available.

Canada Suicide Prevention Service - toll free number 1.833.456.4566. Available 24x7x365.

Crisis Text Line – Text HOME to 686868 in Canada to text with a trained Crisis Responder.

Kids Help Line – Text CONNECT to 686868 from anywhere in Canada, any time, about anything.

Dedication

Dedicated without hesitation or reservation to the love of my life, my wife Sherrie. Thank you for a lifetime of understanding, patience, inspiration and love.

And to my kiddos, Sarah, Benjamin, Jerusha, Nathaniel, and Rebecca. (Y'all are wonderful, but kind of weird children. I think you get it from your mother.)

And to my granddaughter Ella. (You, my dearest, are perfect. I think you get it from your Papa.)

TABLE OF CONTENTS

Preface   1
Forward by Nancy O'Grady   5

CHAPTERS

01. Kabul, Afghanistan, and The Melting Snow   9
02. Memories and Mannequins   17
03. Life on the Mississippi and Papered Windows   21
04. Paper Jesus and Satin Slips   27
05. Ft. Benning, Georgia, and the Mop Bucket   33
06. San Angelo, Texas, and Lawn Mowers   41
07. Intermittent Light and Normality of Darkness   49
08. Ein Gedi, Israel, and Road Trips   53
09. Tombstone, Arizona, and the Blue Chair   59
10. Shilo, Tennessee and Shattered Studies   65
11. Dubai, United Arab Emirates and Watter   71
12. The Berlin Wall and Tampons   77
13. The Green Bean and a Small Step   87
14. Yorkville Village, Toronto, and Ceiling Tiles   95
15. Ballast and Barnacles   101
16. Stockholm and My Own Skin   105
17. The Path Forward and a Perceived End-State   109

➤ ALTARED BOY

PREFACE

This book has been germinating in my soul for over 20 years, but it has only been in the last two years that I have chosen to put pen to paper. My hesitancy has always been the misplaced empathy of not wanting to hurt those who hurt me, and it is still a concern as I attempt to carefully craft every word.

The few I have disclosed my past to have routinely suggested I write a book as a vehicle of personal therapy. I've always dismissed those suggestions, as I viewed writing about myself as a gratuitous and futile effort. What could be gained? What would the end game be? What good would it do? It was then that a close friend reached into the darkness and turned on the light by suggesting that it might help others who have travelled the same path.

And so, I began. The dreaded blank page staring at me, and me staring back. A standoff. Who would break first? One word, and then two. I began to jot down a few words of my different memories in point form. Papered window. Blue chair. Lawnmower. They all had meaning. And the more words I jotted, the more they seemed to connect to other memories I had forgotten. One memory linked inexorably to another, and then another. I ended up with a ruthless and relentless body of flashbacks that must be stitched together into a coherent story.

As I sat looking at the notes that represented the abuse, they triggered memories of other times in my life when I had recalled that same abuse. This pairing became the format by which I tell my story. It is a patchwork quilt of my life. A life that is occasionally and savagely attacked at the most inopportune times by merciless flashbacks. And this is the ongoing curse of those sexually assaulted as young children. The realization that it didn't end there, and it never ends.

You are a different 'you.' One that will never know the 'you' whom you would have been. It is not the end; it is a beginning. It is possible to draw strength from events that were neither your fault nor your creation. It is not ideal, but what in life is? The simple acknowledgement can be a platform for the launch of personal healing, reconciliation with your memories, and even forgiveness. Forgiveness is important, as much to the forgiver as to the forgiven.

    I had an old pair of jeans which had numerous holes in them. (And not in the modern pre-torn fashion statement manner.) They were work jeans and comfortable, so I hated to toss them out. My wife sat one evening and stitched up all the torn spots. Pulling seams together, creating patches, she worked her seamstress magic. The damage was much less noticeable when she passed them back to me. I could wear them again, and they fit well because they were my jeans, formed to me, which had been part of my life for a long time. As I wore them again, I noticed that the strongest part of this garment was the places previously torn apart. Had they never been torn, they would never be this strong.

    David Lewis

FORWARD

By Nancy O'Grady

Almost all my childhood memories involve some aspect of religiosity. My Irish-Catholic father worked overtime to mitigate any untoward influence that my Protestant (subtextual "heathen") mother may have wielded over me and my assured heavenly afterlife. Overcompensation by my father assured that we were a Catholic-and-then-some family, even though my mother did not participate. Elementary school was no-brainer Catholic. With no Catholic secondary school in our town, my classmates and I would eventually be thrust into the public system where it was hoped that our Catholic souls would be adequately equipped to repel most things secular

We were a close-knit group of students that entered Catholic kindergarten together and, in most cases, exited grade eight together. We learned together, played at recess together, went to birthday parties together, passed surreptitious notes when teachers' backs were turned, gossiped together, rode bikes together and amplified our Catholic belief systems when we saw each other at Sunday Mass and sat giggling during weekly Mass in the school library. Didn't everyone in our class live basically the same lives? We attended school, Sunday Mass, we had our First Communions together and we participated in the sacrifice of Confirmation together. We were faithful. We looked up to the priests. Our priests were role models. In ways both spoken and tacit, we learned and never questioned that the Holy Ghost Fathers were deserving of our respect and admiration. Ours was a belief system which provided a constant source of security and comfort for most of us, but in the fullness of time, I learned that such was not the case for all of us.

Some forty years after saying goodbye in June of our grade eight year, it was with unbridled joy and anticipation that a small group of our core grade eight class was able to meet a few years ago for an unofficial reunion of sorts at a local pub. Seven people who had once been so close but for whom the passage of some four decades, geography and simply, life, had made getting together all but impossible. Six of us arrived at the proscribed time and waited. Would Davey Lewis come? We knew he was in the military and often deployed around the world. He had been invited and there was a chance that he might be available. If sheer willing could create an event, then our group's desire to see him and to reconnect with him would will him through the door. He's here. Davey Lewis is here, cutting an impressive figure in his dress white uniform.

In our small group, we noisily talked over each other in our delight to be back together again and to catch up on each other's lives. In a moment that I have lived to regret mightily and for which I have apologized often, I flippantly threw out the following: "So, Dave, you were an altar boy. Were there shenanigans?" The table went silent, the conviviality evaporated and David Lewis took a breath and answered," Yes." I was and am ashamed to have characterized abuse by Catholic priests in our very own church by using a word that one might use to describe a Hallowe'en prank or sneaking into a bar underage.

In his book, Altared Boy, David Lewis attempts and succeeds in no uncertain terms to shine a light on unspeakable, unconscionable and heinous treatment by abusive Catholic priests. Each page delivers a gut-punch. And that all this happened to one of us, one of our favourite little school pals, a boy with whom we spent all our school-based hours for all our formative years, a happy-go-lucky, funny, engaging and entertaining lad? Heartbreaking and pernicious. The reader cannot look away. The reader must not look away.

David Lewis uses flashback to weave chapters of his life together in an exceptionally readable and compelling way. David's ability to connect past trauma to later life choices and to the soundtrack of his adult life will leave the reader with no doubt about the scope of abuse by priests or the deep trauma that inevitably follows the victims for the rest of their lives. His story-telling is riveting. You are there. You hear it. You see it. You must acknowledge it. You must process it.

It is always very challenging and jarring when, as an adult, you are accidentally or become purposely disabused of some of your most sacred and enduring beliefs. If you have not been paying attention to media reports of abuse by Catholic priests or if you have purposely looked away, this book will disrupt you. It will shake you up. It will challenge your beliefs and confront your personal paradigms about the Catholic Church. The way in which the seeds planted in our childhoods become the gardens of our adult lives is inextricably linked to the sum total of our experiences. My childhood friend and schoolmate David Lewis shares with readers the traumatic seeds of betrayal from his childhood experiences and bursts through the tragedy with an encouraging and heartening conclusion. He wishes healing for the wounded, visibility for the suffering and understanding and compassion for the onlookers. Would that all survivors of abuse might emerge as my friend David Lewis has, speaking truth to power, with dignity, with compassion and with an abiding faith in humanity..

Nancy O'Grady

Chapter 1

KABUL, AFGHANISTAN AND THE MELTING SNOW

It was the crusty kind of snow, like a Creme Brule, with a solid but fragile crust on top and a soft, untouched cloud below. We would walk carefully and gingerly across it as children, attempting not to break the 'crust' by sliding our feet to minimize the impact. Sure enough, after every few attempts, you would feel the snow collapse beneath your boot, leaving a single broken footprint cratered behind you. As a nine-year-old boy, this was one of the self-entertaining challenges created during the cold Canadian winters in Woodstock, Ontario.

The expansive lawn on the southwest corner of Dundas and Clarke Streets belonged to St. Rita's Roman Catholic Church and School. This cold Saturday morning, its vast expanse lay buried under this brittle type of snow. Morning mass was over, and my obligations as an altar boy had been concluded for the day. I had a few coins in one pocket, and I would stop on the far corner at Wray's Gas Bar and Diner and buy some penny candy. I loved the smell of the bacon cooking, the toast, the gas, and the cigarette smoke combined to form a wonderful warm respite from the cold. In my other pocket was my childhood's dirty little secret.

I began my trek across the untouched virgin landscape of the crusty snow. Sliding my foot as far as I could, I would gingerly shift my weight, trying not to break the crust and then slide my other foot. If the snow held, I would feel triumph in small victories. Again, I would continue to walk forward carefully. Usually, I would make it a couple of strides before my minimal weight would win, and my little rubber boot would crack the surface of the snow. When I arrived at about the center of the lawn this day, I stopped.

The toe of my boot intentionally banged against the snow, and I kicked at it until I had created a deep little cavern. When I decided my little excavation had sufficient dimensions, I stopped and stared down at it. My hand cradled the object in my jacket pocket, and I was almost afraid to remove it and toss it into the small crater I had created. I felt that the entire world's eyes were upon me. I felt that everyone except for God was watching. The morning was frigid, and I wanted this second-worst part of my day to be over. I still wanted to go to Wray's, and then I had the eight-block walk up the Clarke Street hill to home.

My mother was a devout Catholic with Irish heritage and an O'Connor lineage. If the church were open, we would be there. Obligated by God, the church, but mostly her, we must attend every 'Holy Day of Obligation.' Most mornings, other children were allowed to sleep. Not at our house. My sister and I were up and dressed, standing for mandatory inspection before leaving home. I would wash my face carefully and scrutinize it in the mirror. I loathed the odour of her thumb-applied nicotine-stained saliva on my face if I had missed a spot. Which, unfortunately, I usually did. She was very proud that I was an altar boy. She often volunteered me to serve at the early morning mass before school. I am unsure to this day if it was for Christs' sake, the church's sake, my sake, or I suspect her sake as a perceived holy mother who could raise such a devout young man. I would bundle up and trudge through the snow to fulfill my obligations. Today was one of those obligatory days.

I stared at the pocket I had created in the snow as I reached into my coat pocket. I took the small bundle I had wrapped in multiple layers of brown paper towels from the church bathroom and quickly tossed it down. A few moments of kicking and scooping snow with my boots concealed my little excavation, along with its contents. This lawn was vast, and no one would ever discover my secret.

The walk home was noticeably colder without my underwear. But this was the only solution my adolescent mind conceived. I was embarrassed by the bloodstains and was afraid to try to explain. On laundry day, my mother would again undoubtedly go into another tirade about how my underwear keeps disappearing, how she keeps having to buy more. The berating would subside when she would eventually blame the washer or dryer vortex, which also apparently consumed socks. I would stand silently, once again staring at the ground, agree, or shrug my shoulders.

It's October, and an uncommon rain pummels my armoured SUV as our convoy rolls back towards Kabul. The three vehicles in convoy are almost identical. Large, black and many times heavier than the original factor editions. Much of the weight comes from the thick steel panels in the floor, the doors and throughout the frame. The original windows had been replaced with almost 1-inch-thick bulletproof glass, and there are strategic gun ports at various locations. A tall beige column protrudes up from the roof of each. When we leave Camp Eggers or head anywhere outside the wire, we stand the column up, secure it, and 'turn on the music.' The apparatus sends out a signal which jams radios and cell phones in the close vicinity of the convoy. It makes most things that could be detonated with a radio signal ineffectual, at least while we pass by. Today I am in the middle vehicle seated behind the driver, with Australian Sarah next to me.

The bulk of our mission in-country is to document the efforts, progress, and success of members of all 34 coalition countries. We have five vehicles in total and usually about 16-

20 troops. Almost every day, we roll with someone. Three vehicles and personnel will move with the Italian Army, documenting them as they teach hand-to-hand combat to Afghan National Army (ANA). Two vehicles will proceed to Mazar a Sharif with Australian Army Medics to open a women's clinic for Afghan families and inoculate infants. Sometimes we roll in other convoys. Today Kat is flying with General Caldwell in his Soviet-era helicopter as he goes about his business. Beaver and Liz are in the Canadian RCMP convoy as they teach and mentor Afghan National Police (ANP).

We have spent most of our day and the bulk of the evening with British troops as they train ANA members on a night-time live-fire range. It's been another incredibly long, hot, tiring day that's already at the 19-hour mark. When we get back to Eggers, there is a considerable volume of work to do. Processing imagery and video, running B-roll, dubbing, bi-lines and articles, and then grabbing some horizontal time before heading back out tomorrow. We've developed a reasonably detailed timetable for posting stories and videos. Deadlines for filing and uploading are different for posting the Australian Medic story to the Sydney Morning Herald and 23 other Australian Newspapers than uploading the Italian story to 30-40 papers in Italy. Thank God for 'Chicken-Little.' A young scrawny, incredibly organized American corporal whose job is to file all content overnight. Taxpayers in each of the 34 coalition countries must understand the good things their tax dollars and troops are doing in this country. And why occasionally, their flag may be at half-mast here on base.

The darkness around us is greatly diminished as we head into the flickering lights of Kabul. Melsi, my friend and Albanian Army Captain, is riding shotgun. He blasts Cyndi Lauper's 'Girls Just Wanna Have Fun' on his iPod, and I couldn't think of a less appropriate music choice. But the four of us in the vehicle are loudly and with extreme motivation singing along.

Our collection of vehicles snakes its way as quickly as possible into the clusterf*ck of Kabul traffic. We must travel as closely and rapidly as possible, keeping convoy integrity by maintaining a narrow gap between our vehicles, eliminating the convoy's possibility to be compromised. It isn't an easy task on a good day. Still, it is particularly challenging in the rain at night with limited visibility. Allowing a gap between the SUVs creates the real opportunity for insurgents to insert their vehicles between ours, often with deadly consequences.

As is too often the case, in a city with millions of cars and no traffic laws, no traffic lights and no traffic lanes, we get bogged down to a dead stop. We pull forward enough to bump the convoy vehicle ahead of us physically. This action ensures there is no room for anyone to walk between us. Pedestrian-born IEDs (Improvised Explosive Devises) have been used frequently to devastating effects. Sitting still, trapped in

Masoud Circle in a horizontal Jenga of hundreds of cars, trucks, mopeds, donkey carts and motorbikes, with no avenue for an immediate escape, leaves you incredibly and uncomfortably vulnerable. The rain is hitting my window with a vengeance. Our senses are on edge as every movement around us is suspect. Every moped weaving through stalled traffic in our direction is suspicious. I need to be watching. I need to be aware of everything and everyone around this vehicle.

    I stare out my window and see the snowy lawn at St. Rita's. It is early spring, and the snow is begining to melt. We had been at the afternoon St. Patrick's Day bazaar, and now we were heading home. It was raining hard, and my mother had packed our blue Rambler station wagon with every kid possible to deliver back to our neighbourhood. The scent of 1960's yellow rubber raincoats permeated the vehicle as condensation from hot, sweaty kids built up on the inside of the window. I reach up with my hand and wipe some of the moisture away. My heart goes into panic mode.

    There, not too far from the road, in a small island of grass between the melting snow, was the bright white bundle of my underwear. Remnants of the brown paper towels were on the grass around them. And this wasn't the only such bundle I had hidden in the snow on that yard. There were others out there still hidden, waiting to detonate into my life. I knew my mother would look sideways and see them. I knew she would scream, 'there's your underwear!' I knew she would recognize them as mine and yell for answers I couldn't give. I knew all the other kids would stare at me. I could feel the tears welling in my eyes. My face was flushed and hot, and my heart was pounding in my temples. My panic was at a near nausea-inducing level. The other children laughed and chatted their inane drivel as my heart raced. And then the traffic light changed, and my mother drove casually up the hill.

The convoy lurched ahead a few feet. Cyndi was still singing. The rain was subsiding, and I could see an elderly Afghan gentleman in a small truck next to me. He smiled. I nodded.

I need to get my head back in the game here.

Chapter 2

MEMORIES AND MANNEQUINS

Memory [mem-uh-ree]

noun, plural mem·o·ries.

-   the mental capacity or faculty of retaining and reviving facts, events, impressions, etc., or of recalling or recognizing previous experiences.
-   the act or fact of retaining and recalling impressions, facts, etc.; remembrance; recollection:
-   the length of time over which recollection extends:
-   a mental impression retained; a recollection:

I have always had a reasonably good memory.

My earliest memory is of my lying on a blanket on a lawn, and I feel the satin trim around the edge and touching the warm grass just beyond. It is a corner lot, the house on the left is grey shingle board, and the lawn itself is a foot or so higher than the sidewalk. A red firetruck turns the corner. I remember no siren, as I recall having no fear. I shared those memories in later years with my mother, who was amazed to recognize my house description. We had left that home well before my first birthday.

Dozens of other memories and images of that era survive. They are tucked away in the dusty bankers-boxes in my mind. On those occasions, when I carefully open one of those boxes, searching for an individual photo, other images tumble out onto the table. My father is working on the white Oldsmobile as my sister and I bounce on the large rear seat he had removed and placed on the grass. Another vision of army trucks pulling up in front of our home in Petawawa and my father returning, turning his kit bag upside down and dumping Smarties boxes onto the living room floor. Aunt Lois and cartoon-faced eggcups. Images in my mind of driving my toy cars in the pattern on the art-deco linoleum on the floor. All memories from before my second birthday.

Memories define us. They remind us that cinnamon toast is good, and broccoli is terrible. 'Chip Gramma' gives dry kisses, and 'Sock Gramma' gives wet ones. Like building a paper-mache character, each strand of wet newspaper retains the original imprinted text. All is still there, still readable layer under layer, constructing who we are and slowly and methodically defining us.

I do not have the training to speak about memories, abuse, trauma, or the suppression of memories. I know that many of my memories are not available to me. Memories are suppressed within me, even though I have no recollection of actively deciding to subdue them. They remain hidden just under the surface, waiting for a trigger. They seem to reappear at so many stages and inconvenient junctures of my life. For years I said (and believed) that I wasn't affected by them. 'Strength in adversity,' and other such banal platitudes.

I did not comprehend that I had been burglarized. I have been broken into. Someone had embezzled my future and abducted me with it. The cherubic me had been replaced with a damaged, second-hand, defiled mannequin that would now forever stand in my place. The surrogate me I must now recognize as myself.

Who was the person I would have been?

What was the future I would have had?

What life course would I have followed?

What happy thoughts were amputated from my future memories?

Those who represented themselves as emissaries of angels became the envoys of darkness. They opened windows they didn't give a damn to close and ripped doors off their hinges, leaving them ajar so that winged creatures might enter into my night?

      Everything they stole from me; they took when I was a child.

      Such is my story.

Chapter 3

LIFE ON THE MISSISSIPPI AND PAPERED WINDOWS

Living in New Orleans is (I'm guessing) much like living in Niagara Falls or Las Vegas. There are large areas of the town which are relinquished to tourists and avoided at all costs. The Quarter in New Orleans, the actual Falls in Niagara, or the strip in Vegas is the type of place you go if your family from out of town are visiting. Then you make the obligatory pilgrimage to all the local sights and landmarks. I rarely went to the French Quarter. The scents of bad body odour, beer, vomit and urine are just not the draw they used to be. If I did head to the Quarter, it would be on a Sunday morning to go to one of the cafés around Jackson Square in the shadow of Saint Louis Cathedral. There I would find a table in the sun, a few sugar-dusted beignets, and a steep espresso amid a noticeable lack of drunk tourists.

People think that New Orleans sits where the Mississippi River flows into the Gulf of Mexico. It's almost

100 miles by boat further down the river past Pilottown, where you finally break free of the silt and enter the gulf.

I've always cared about history, and I've always felt links to memories of past times and places. The American Civil War has always commanded a significant and melancholic section of my psyche. I have an emotional attachment to the era, and there's no reason why. Mystics or new agers might relate it to past lives or soul imprinting. Myself, I cease to analyze it and just roll with it and the comfortable familiarity it provides.

So, when in 2001, I stumbled upon the opportunity, and offer, to become the Chief Steward of the Mississippi Queen, I jumped at the change. The 'MQ' was the largest paddlewheel-driven river steamboat ever built when she first floated in 1976. She had 206 staterooms for a capacity of 412 guests and a crew of 157. She gave 3 to 11-day cruises in various sections of the river from New Orleans, 1600 miles up the Mississippi River, to St. Paul, Minnesota. Different times of the year were for other parts of the river system. Memphis, Vicksburg, Hannibal, Baton Rouge, St. Louis were all offered. At Cairo Point, Illinois, we would sometimes head up the Ohio River, the Cumberland, or the Tennessee River. I loved the Civil War-themed cruises more than the Blues, Jazz, or Dixieland cruises.

The beauty of living on the river was, in part, the tranquility of being away from the city's noise and rumblings.

Sitting at twilight on the top deck with the sunset illuminating the river and the giant red paddlewheel churning and propelling us from behind, campfires, parks, and small towns dotting the riverbank always transported me back to a simpler time. Removed from the lights of cities, churning upriver in the dark, the canopy of stars was almost unimaginably bright as it illuminated the night.

When we docked at our various port-of-calls, passengers would head off to Mark Twain's House or Indian Joes Cave in Hannibal, Missouri. Oak Alley Plantation in Vacherie, Vicksburg Battlefield, the Magnolia Pageant in Natchez or whatever shore tour attracted them. During these few hours, we, as the crew, had the freedom to explore independently.

My first time in Baton Rouge was intriguing. The more distant history of Baton Rouge, or 'Red Stick,' originated (as the story goes) from the name French-Canadian explorers gave a large, bloodied cypress pole. It stood on a bluff on the east bank of the river. The 'stick' had once been a large tree that divided the territory between the two indigenous tribes, the Houma Indian Tribe and the Bayougoula Indian Tribe. The tree had long been used to clean pelts, dry game and fish, and on which the flow of blood had stained the wood a crimson red. The sustained blood over the years had killed the tree and had left only the giant tree trunk stained red—a baton rouge.

I recently read on the flamboyant and maverick Depression-era governor of Louisiana, Huey Long. I was interested in exploring downtown and, notably, the State Capital Building, Governor Longs' assassination location. A few fellow crewmembers shared my interest, and we headed off to explore.

I was used to small riverfront towns being shuttered and neglected, but I was not ready for the extent to which a city this size showed signs of abandonment. Block after block of once vibrant shops had now decayed into peeling paint, rusted signage, and shuttered stores, many with brown paper taped to the inside of the glass storefront, blocking all views.

The brown paper was new and taped to the little glass window on the door leading into the vestry at St Rita's. The vestry is the small room where the priest would put on his vestments to perform the mass, and the altar boys would don their cassocks. Sometimes wearing my cassock, I would pretend in my mind that I was a priest. I wanted to be a priest, or at least what my mother told me I wanted.

The first time we played the 'tickle game,' I was instructed to put both hands on the wall. The vestry walls were wood panels, and they had the scent of years of stale air and incense. I could smell it as I stared at the wood grain pattern between my small hands pressed against the wall. The game was not to move as Father Schmid tugged my shirt out of my pants. His cold fingers would tickle my belly, and I would twitch and pull away. He would admonish me that that wasn't how we played the game. Again, his hands would travel down into the back of my pants and then around the front. I would stare at the wood grain and try desperately to play the game correctly, telling myself, 'Don't move, don't move.'

As always, when mass was over, and we would head off the altar, back into the vestry, I would try to get out of my cassock as quickly as possible and be gone. I was not quick enough to exit most of the time before he locked the doors. And then his hands. Always his hands. Sometimes when I was pulling the cassock over my head, I would feel him already touching me.

The 'tickle game' progressed beyond tickles. The doors were locked by him to prevent our encounters from being interrupted, or discovered. I had no avenue of retreat. This time however, as I entered the vestry to do my duty as an altar boy, I noticed that he had blocked out the little glass window in the door with brown paper. My heart began to beat faster. Even as a child, I could see the signs that indicated an escalation. My stomach ached as only those trapped in an inescapable abyss could understand. My hopes rested only on the expectation that it would be over quickly, not on the chance that it wouldn't occur.

"Lewis! Are you coming? Dude, the store is closed. I snapped back to the present and the hot Louisiana sun. "Why are you staring at the window?" My friends were now a ways ahead of me and are looking back, confused by my actions. I am unsure how long I've been staring at the brown-papered glass. The hot Louisiana sun is brutal, but it has nothing to do with how profusely I am sweating. A cool breeze off the river offers me the only redemption I can expect.

"Coming," I yell, bounding off towards them, with one last glance back at the papered window.

Chapter 4

PAPER JESUS AND SATIN SLIPS

Saturday morning, watching cartoons, there would always be the inevitable line of gunpowder burning along, unstoppable towards an enormous pile of explosives. Memories can be that way. Something sparks a thought – a smell – a taste - that ignites a time or place deep within your subconscious. That fire begins to burn, and as it moves towards you, its light creates shadows, briefly and ominously flickering in your mind. Occasionally one detonates and explodes with monstrous internal violence, establishing clarity before wafting away, reduced to a dangerous poisonous vapour floating just above the surface.

The abused do not question whether abuse has imprinted their life; every day somehow reminds them that it has. It has reached so deeply into their soul that it has been etched forever into their DNA. Like a hereditary genetic disorder, abuse maintains a malignancy on their spirit.

My self-worth was determined at a very early age. When I undressed to get in the bathtub or into my pajamas and caught a glimpse of myself in the mirror, I knew that I had value. I calmly recognized what the transactional currency of my worth was. I might not have liked it, it might have hurt, but it was better than being nothing. Any misgivings I had, even then, were unquestionably my fault.

I was the problem in the equation. It was simply inconceivable that a priest could be wrong or do wrong. In the forced litany of actions and responses, if someone was defective, was it the man of God or stupid little me?

My parents' marriage was reasonably horrific, and I have no recollection of kindness, love, or tenderness between them. My father was a sailor for many years in the Royal Canadian Navy, and he transferred his military acquired knowledge as an electrician to a civilian career after leaving the forces. My mother held great pride and boasted about having a Grade 5 education. She would tell of being pulled out of school during the great depression to look after ailing relatives. She would often speak of the great tug-of-war. Of the wonderful nuns pulling to keep her in class and of her inebriated harlot mother pulling to take her away.

She found solace and purpose, and identity in suffering, and the church.

She was a good mother in many ways. When anything was happening at school, she was there. Any class presentation, play, choral rendition, Christmas program, she was there, front and center, visible to all. She was the best, most supportive mother, unlike the other kids' mothers, and definitely unlike her mother. We were lucky to have her, and we best not forget that. She knew it, we knew it, and every teacher and the principal for sure knew it.

My father was much less present in my life, and I imagine in hindsight that my mother had intentionally orchestrated this. She needed 100% of my sister and my affection, and she wasn't willing to share, not even with him. Her desired narrative of being a single mother, suffering through the constant unyielding stream of sacrifices elevated her to a distinction she otherwise wouldn't have achieved.

I am the father of five wonderful kids and the grandfather of one beautiful little peanut granddaughter. She's still a little too young to hold on for horsey rides up and down the hallway, but I recently got on my hands and knees and chased her a bit. One of my few memories of my dad ever playing was with my sister Kerrie and me on his back, him making horsey noises and galloping down the hallway with us laughing and screaming. It lasted for maybe a hallway and back until my mother came screaming around the corner, physically pulling us off his back. Screaming ensued between them. God forbid he should be the recipient of our affection.

They didn't fight non-stop, just all the time. It's a fascinating study of how sadness and conflict can become so common in your life that it almost becomes comforting. Whether it was the hands of the priest on me or the hellacious strife between my parents, there was solace in what was familiar.

As a child, I would wake up in the night and lay there quietly, in my Daniel Boone pajamas, listening in the darkness. Within moments I would usually hear the muffled tones of a heated argument from the kitchen. There was some comfort in the routine that all was as it was supposed to be. I would roll over and go back to sleep. Sometimes when I got up in the morning, I would ask, "Where's daddy" she would reply, "he's gone."

For weeks or months at a time, they would split up. My mother enjoyed playing the struggling single mother card when my father was gone. She was a saint. No seriously. She was a saint and would concoct scenarios to validate her canonization. For Easter one year, my sister and I made her a crucifix. I took a wooden board and, with a small handsaw, fashioned a rugged and somewhat uneven cross. Kerrie drew a little Jesus on paper, complete with a bloody crown of thorns, side puncture and blood marks on hands and feet. Then together, we went to the workbench in the basement and taking the cut-out of her drawn figure, we nailed it to the cross. We both beamed with pride over what we had created for her.

She did adore it and hung it in a place of pride on the kitchen wall. We, at the time, were unaware of its mystical powers. All of this occurred during a period when my dad was absent. Within a few days of receiving and mounting the crucifix, my sister and I woke up during the night. My mother was loudly whispering that we needed to come and pray. Staggering down the hall in our pajamas, she told us of the miracle. She had gotten up in the night for water and noticed the cross was on the table, not the wall. She hung it back up, had her water, and then sat in the living room. On sitting down, she heard a noise in the kitchen. Rising, she saw the cross again on the table. Questioning to herself whether she had rehung the item, she once again carefully hooked it over the nail. Once again, she heard the same noise in the living room and returned to the kitchen. This time she was startled to see it once more on the table. As she went to retrieve it, a bright light shone down on her, and she heard a voice from heaven say, "My Daughter." She explained the importance to us as, up until this time, God only had one child, a son.

The cross was standing on the sofa. She, my sister, and I knelt in front and said the rosary over and over until daybreak. Later that day, she took it to the rectory to have it blessed. She was gone for a long time.

Canonization was imminent, no doubt, once someone notified the Pope.

As always, my life's situation determined that those around me were righteous, pious, anointed, and holy individuals and that I, as a child, should aspire to be like them. Any hesitancy, doubt or shame on my part was only because of my degraded condition and my need for penance.

A few weeks later, I applied the same logic when I arrived home from grade school, and Father Schmid was in his underwear in our living room, and my mom was barefoot in only her satin slip.

Chapter 5

FORT BENNING, GEORGIA AND THE MOP BUCKET

I sat about midway back on the bus. My newly issued duffle bag, green, with U.S. ARMY stenciled on the side, sat propped vertically on my lap. The Battle Dress Uniform, or BDU I was wearing, still had the 'new clothing' fold marks. My boots had never really seen dirt, and my camo BDU cap slid easily over my new shorn hair. The olive-drab bus snaked its way through the hot, humid Georgia night.

A quiet, tense foreboding hung in the air like the Spanish moss hung from the trees. The scent of 50 nervous and sweating recruits mixed with the American south's pine thicket and magnolia scent. Onward we rolled deeper into the darkness towards our precarious future.

I caught the stench of the sweltering asphalt as the bus took a hard left onto a seemingly deserted parking lot. For a moment, I thought I saw the headlights pan across a group of about 20 large men in uniforms, wearing Smokey-the-Bear hats. As quickly as I saw them, they seemed to disappear. The bus lurched to a stop, grunted, shivered, and then sat ominously quiet. My heart raced. Sixty pairs of eyes looked at each other, squinted to see out the window, a few tears began to form. We sat. Waiting. Waiting.

The door at the front of the bus opened.

I could barely see the single individual climb the few stairs and turn to face his waiting victims in the darkness. There he stood. He was an enormous colossus of a man. He stood slightly hunched over as his massive frame would not fit this standard-size bus. His eyes almost glowed as he spoke the gentle and supportive words, "You maggots have exactly 20 seconds to get the fuck off this bus, and God help the last man off!"

I was not positioned to be the first man off, but I would not be the last from my placement on the bus. I wrapped the straps of my duffle bag around my arm, stood up, and began to swing it mercilessly back and forth like a canvas battering ram. I knocked the less aggressive occupants back into their seats as I pushed forward towards the unknown. Finally, I turned and stepped down the few bus stairs and out into the night. I watched my new boots step out onto the sticky asphalt and looked up to see a long gauntlet of at least a dozen screaming, vein-bulging faces. Each one was yelling, louder and more animated than the other. They called me various low-life forms, questioned my sexual orientation, called my mother's moral character into question, and forecasted my overall demise. The final link in the reception committee to hades instructed me with significant volume to run across the field towards the light. MOVE! MOVE! MOVE!

Having no idea where I was heading, I tossed my duffel bag up on my shoulders and began running. All around me, there were already casualties. Duffle bags, pieces of kit, exhausted recruits, guys with twisted or broken ankles littered the grass like a medieval battlefield. I dodged and leaped over the carnage as I ran blindly.

Once at the light, I realized I was amidst a group of decrepit barracks huddled together in the dark. I was being screamed at again to get into a military formation. STAND HERE! DROP YOUR KIT! I did as instructed, and then I looked up. Immediately my eyes caught the gaze of a drill sergeant. ARE YOU LOOKING AT ME?! YOU LOOKING AT ME, YOU F***ING MAGGOT! He ran towards me, face to face inches from me, the brim of his hat hitting my forehead as he yelled. I could feel the spit from his jeering hitting my face and mouth. I stared ahead, intentionally unfocused, standing firm. He moved on to another victim.

The verbal annihilation continued well into the night. Hour after hour. At one point, in the wee hours of the morning, the troop in front of me went down on one knee and vomited onto the red Georgia clay. As his mother was not present, the drill sergeant offered his compassion by demanding to know why he had desecrated his parade field with his vomit. Who had permitted the troops to puke? Forever engraved in my mind is the young private in his new green uniform, ordered to pick up his vomit and put it in his pocket. I watched him. Vomit, mixed with red Georgia clay, ran between his fingers as he dropped handfuls into his pocket.

Such was my induction to the U.S. Army, Infantry Basic Training at Ft. Benning Georgia in the summer of 1985.

The first few days of intense 'acclimation' and purging soon gave way to months of challenging but rewarding physical fitness, instruction, and weapons training. Drill Sergeant Mossley, the colossus from the bus, became a trustworthy, caring but firm mentor to his trainees' platoon. As a group, we went from an 'I'm going to die' mentality to a 'Hell yes, I can do this' mindset. Days of learning to fire NATO and Warsaw Pact weapons, assemble and detonate claymore mines, and stand perfectly still in a foxhole while an M60 tank drives over your position. There was disarming of anti-personnel mines and learning military codes of conduct which were offset with relaxing nights of mopping, buffing, shining boots and barracks maintenance.

It was my night to mop between 0200 and 0300. The barracks at the Harmony Church section of Ft Benning were built quickly during WWII to house the massive influx of new troops training before heading to the battlefield. Forty years later, it was my temporary home for 14 weeks of Basic Training, followed by 14 weeks of Advanced Infantry Training. The age-worn linoleum was missing in many areas of the floor, but it still needed to be mopped, waxed, buffed every single night. I filled the yellow bucket with hot water from the tap in the communal shower and dumped in a liberal amount of pine sol. I began a wet, sloshy pattern across the floor.

    "Davey! Davey!" I turned from my wet, sloshy pine-sol-infused pattern on the floor of St. Rita's basement hall. Esther Peto, the elderly cleaning lady, was calling to me from across the room, standing in the doorway of the church kitchen. She had maintained the janitorial needs of the church ever since Moses had climbed down out of the mountains. She was aged enough now that she hired me for $10 every Saturday morning to do the more cumbersome jobs. I'm not sure my small frame was much more capable than her older one, but I persisted. I stuck the mop head in the draining basket, gave it a quick press, and headed to the kitchen. Esther, who was never in possession of a sunny disposition, seemed even more irritated than usual. "You're needed upstairs," she barked at me. On climbing the back stairs, the screen door opened, and Father Schmid was standing there. I followed him across the small parking lot to the rectory's back door.

Upon entering the rectory, you immediately arrived in a small office with desk and bookshelves, where any parish priests would meet with or counsel church members. Turning to the left was the small kitchen where Bessie, the cook and housekeeper, prepared breakfast. As a cook, she had sailed on the Ark with Noah. In the parish hierarchy of the Old Testament Matriarchs, she held seniority over Esther.

As I followed the father through the kitchen, Bessie's skeletal figure made an overt point to look at me with disgust. In the short passage, she managed to look me up and down, shake her head, and 'harumph' her disgust loud enough to make sure I heard. With my options severely limited, I averted her eyes and stared towards the floor as I followed along.

Upstairs were the priests' private rooms. They were sparsely decorated with a dresser, single bed, thin mattress, and mandatory crucifix so that the crucified Christ could watch any proceedings. I hated the bedroom. I hated the smell of the mattress, and I hated how the bristles of the whiskers of the shaved face would scrape my thighs. I much preferred the simple 'tickle game.'

Mercifully, it didn't take long. I would stare at the ceiling or the crucifix, watching 'him' watching me. I would wonder about so many things, but before I was revealed any celestial answers, the liturgy of lust would be completed, and I would be almost angrily dismissed. I hated the walk alone back down the stairs and through the kitchen. I was afraid of Skeletor and her open display of loathing towards me. A tray of bacon passed my eyes, and I wanted a piece. I wanted to reach for it and run. But as many trips as I made through that kitchen, I never did.

      I headed back to the church basement to finish my mopping. I descended the stairs and turned into the small kitchen. Esther was sitting at the small table with her cup of tea. She stared at me in silence for an uncomfortable amount of time. "Here, go to Timmies and get me an Old-Fashioned donut, and get yourself whatever donut you want." She slid two quarters across the table towards me.

      The half-block walk to the donut shop was full of thoughts I chose not to think. Filled with questions, I refused to ask. The smell of the donut shop with its bright yellow counter and row of customers sitting on the red stools was always welcome. I stood in line between two flannel-clad gentlemen three times my height.

      Back in the kitchen, I sat in silence across from Esther and could feel her eyes upon me. She pulled her donut into small pieces and ate them separately. My chocolate-dipped delicacy melted in my mouth. I wondered even then if the donut was a gift of compassion or a token for services rendered, but it tasted the same. My mop awaited me where I had left it. The water was cold now, but it would still do the job. And doing the job was important.

The strong pine-sol scent filled the barracks. I quietly and quickly mopped around the base of each bunk with its cargo of sleeping soldiers. The next troop was designated to buff the floors, and he arrived soon after I finished mopping. I rinsed the mop and hung it in its place, dumped the bucket and retired to my rack for the tiny amount of sleep recruits were allowed to have. I lay there awake for a long time, once again staring at the ceiling.

Chapter 6

SAN ANGELO, TEXAS AND THE LAWN MOWER

I was married in the first few days of 1980. A new decade. A new life. I am still married to the same lovely little Texas lady, more from her enduring patience than my enduring value. We were young, too young to be getting married. We both look back with the same realization. The wisdom that 40+ years, five kids, and so far, one grandbaby can provide.

We met because I was hitchhiking through the area. I had just finished the first year of college, and a classmate and I had decided to hitchhike from Windsor, Ontario, to California. We hatched the plan over a few idea-inspiring beverages. No stone was left unturned in the preparation of this endeavour. We would thumb across the country, arrive in California, live on the beach, drink beverages with beautiful blonde California girls, have a great tan, and life would be good. Done. We left the bar at the Killarney Hotel and headed over the Ambassador Bridge into Detroit.

Dozens of rides later, the inner city gave way to the Midwest's grasslands and rolling hills. We had not a care in the world. We sat with our legs dangling down towards traffic on the rail of an interstate overpass in Chicago, sharing a jug of juice and a joint. In Kansas City, when a pick-up pulled over to give us a ride, we both jumped into the bed of the truck. As the driver pulled swiftly away, we realized there was no tailgate on the vehicle as we were both slid quickly out onto the asphalt road.

The two US Coast Guard guys in the Mercedes had a fishing tackle box full of drugs they had confiscated during their duties. They shared pretty generously.

And there were the 'Cheech and Chong' fedora-wearing dudes in the beat-up Chevelle coming south out of Des Moines, Iowa. When they pulled over and picked us up, we jumped in the back seat full of large green garbage bags and a thick pot cloud. They said they were heading to Oregon. We looked at each other, Oregon being a long way due west of Des Moines, and they were heading south. Oh well, we wanted to go south; silence is golden. As they pulled back onto the interstate, they mentioned that the bags all around us were all filled with pot, and we were more than welcome to fill the little zip-lock they passed us. Done. My buddy opened one of the stuffed green trash bags, and, sure enough, it was packed with weed. Just as he had the bag wide open, there was a loud bang as the front driver-side tire blew! Everyone jumped, and the green herbal went everywhere.

The driver tried to get the speeding car under control as it heaved from side to side on the highway. With every sideways heave, loose marijuana flew in the air. Surprisingly 'Cheech' got the vehicle under control and pulled over on the gravel shoulder. The interior of the car was blanketed in green. It was on the dashboard, the seats, their shoulders, and lap, even on the brims of their fedoras. We wished them good luck as we quickly exited the vehicle. They fired up a pre-rolled joint to help them relax after the near wreck. We got out of there as soon as possible and headed down the shoulder away from the vehicle. We were about a quarter-mile away when an Iowa state trooper pulled in behind them. Our next ride pulled over to pick us up as we saw the trooper walking up to the driver's side window. I do not know what happened to those two fine gentlemen, but I'm sure it wasn't good.

Hitch-hiking across the country is draining. Entertaining but exhausting. We waited in a cornfield next to a small Motor-court motel watching for people to check out, so we could run and use their showers and shampoos. But enough was enough. We headed to Texas, where his brother was a Baptist preacher, to get clean and rested for a few days before our final push to a life of sin and decadence in California! This fate landed me in San Angelo, where I would meet the little Texas gal with whom I would share my life.

One of our first homes in San Angelo was right next door to my in-laws. Convenient for a young 20's couple who had very little to their name, particularly a lawnmower. Now granted, there's not a lot of need for lawnmowers in West Texas in the summer. The grass is more of a garden than a lawn. What begins looking soft and green in the spring tends to turn into a crunchy brown angel hair pasta full of sharp skin-piercing stickers in the summer. Before it reached the angel-hair stage, I decided to mow our lawn.

The lawnmower was in the back corner of the garage. There wasn't a lot of grass, just a small lawn between St. Rita's church building and the rectory. My small arms struggled to pull it out and negotiate the boxes, crates, and other items on the dirty concrete floor. As I pushed it out into the hot summer sun, I could see my mother and Father Schmid standing on the wooden stoop at the door of the rectory.

After a few tries, it became evident that my skinny chicken-wing arms didn't possess the strength to get this mower going. I stood back in familiar failure while Fr Schmid came down and fired it up. It was a hard push as I made the first of many passes. On my way back, I could see my mother motioning to me and her arms flailing around her head. I stood there watching her, confused on many levels, but finally understood her instructions to 'take your shirt off.' I didn't want to, and I shook my head no. After a bit of back and forth, I could feel tears welling up inside my petite frame. I stared at my sneakers.

I was hard-headed, I guess a little slow. Father Schmid came down from the wooden stoop and chatted with me about whether children should obey their mothers. I knew they should, and I knew better than to disobey. I removed my shirt and handed it to him. I watched him return to the stoop where my mom had been and hang it over the wooden railing. Where did my mom go? With a wave of his hand, he instructed me to continue mowing.

Back and forth, back and forth, I pushed the lawnmower over that small patch of grass. With every pass, the hot summer sun made me sweatier and sweatier. At one point, Fr Schmid appeared with a small glass of lemonade. I stood gulping it while he commented on my sweat and mopped it with the palm of his hand around my lower back. The lemonade was gone too soon. After a few more passes, I finished the lawn. I could see my shirt still hanging where he had placed it, and I wanted to run and grab it and keep running.

Beads of sweat ran down my chicken chest, arms, and the hollow of my bareback into my undershorts. Bits of mown grass was itchy as they stuck to the sweat. I turned off the mower and pushed it towards the garage. As I turned the corner, I could see him out of the corner of my eye, coming down the few wooden steps from his observation post. The lawnmower went back in the corner, in the shadows. Those shadows were neither my friend nor my enemy, just my intimate acquaintances. Those shadows on a hot summer afternoon, in the back corner, hid me, hid him, hid us. From those shadows, I could see cars passing by on Dundas Street. As his hands pulled my pants to my ankles, I wondered about the people in those cars. As his hands explored the hot sweat in every corner and crevice of my body, I wondered where those people passing by were going. I didn't like the smell of his sweat. I didn't like the taste. How could all those people just be driving past?

    The heat in the back corner was worse than outside. The air was stifling, and it smelled of gas, oil and old wood. I was thankful when it was over. I wanted my shirt. I wanted to put it back on, but I wanted first to wipe off my chest. I pulled the shirt from the wooden rail. Once on, it stuck to my frail wet body. I looked back at the open garage but saw only shadows. Our car was still in the parking lot, so I walked up the stairs and into the church. And she was there. I dipped my fingers in the holy water and crossed myself. Walking to the pew she was in, I genuflected and kneeled beside her. She whispered, as to not offend God, "are you done?" "Did you get it all mowed?" I nodded. We left. On the way home, she bought me an orange popsicle. I knew I could fit most of it in my mouth. It was cold and welcome and helped get rid of the taste. I hate orange popsicles to this day, but I still like lemonade. Go figure.

"You should take your shirt off," my wife said as I started to mow our meagre Texas lawn. I ignored her. I pretended I couldn't hear her over the mower. In the corner of my eye, I could see her making hand motions. I turned the mower off. "You should take your shirt off," she said again. "I don't want to," was my reply. "If I were a guy, I'd take my shirt off in this heat," she announced. "I SAID I DON'T WANT TO!" and just like that, something that should have been simple and nice turned into shit. She went into the house confused and sad, and I finished the lawn angry and alone.

Once again, wounds from the past, silently festering just below the surface, rear up and infect those around you.

Chapter 7

INTERMITTANT LIGHT AND THE NORMALITY OF DARKNESS

St. Rita's was a good church to grow up in, apart from the personal pedophilic sexual abuse. It was a self-identified 'Irish' parish with a predominance of second and third-generation Irish immigrant families. The aristocracy of the parish were the McKerrals, two families of the O'Grady brothers, two families of the O'Regan brothers, the Kenny's, the Lynchs, the Carrolls and others. 'T'was' a grand enclave of the old sod, ministered to by the heavily Irish-populated Holy Ghost or Spiritan Fathers.

The year's big event was always the St. Patrick's Day bazaar. The church basement was transformed into a small patch of Kerry, Cork, or Donegal. Crepe-paper shamrocks would festoon the archways leading into an 'outdoor' tea garden offering tiny green-bread finger sandwiches and Irish breakfast tea. There were games for children, silent auctions, sale tables of used books, kitchen items, toys, and whatnots. And of course, my mother and Mrs. Kenny always had the small gift shop at the bottom of the stairs open during this time. It was full of rosaries, crucifixes, statues of the saints, medals, scapulars and other various catholic nick-nacks, paddywhacks and thingamajigs. All in all, it was great fun.

I communicate this because I want to present an accurate, balanced, and multi-faceted story of my experience. There were good times and good people. I had friends, played at recess, laughed, played dodgeball with the mandatory big red rubber balls that every school in the 60s had. I ate lunch, shared snacks, sang in the children's choir, painted in art class, and played army with Mark, Peter, and Danny.

The abuse, the rape, was just an accepted part of life. Was it supposed to be different? I had no metric by which to judge these things. I didn't like it, but there were many things an eight-year-old boy didn't like. I didn't like broccoli, liver and onions, or chores like taking out the trash on a cold winter night. It was not until a lifetime later that I realized this was not a normal part of growing up. It was way too many years after that I began to recognize the impact the abuse had inflicted upon me.

I liked being around Father Roach, Father McCarthy, Father Cunningham, Father Brennan, and even grumpy elderly Father McCormick. They were remarkable men, a wholesome male influence, and they were only ever kind and understanding. I always think of Father Cunningham in the center of the dodge ball circle, sticking his tongue out, laughing, challenging all the kids, and the 8-10 balls hitting him at once. We battered him from all sides with the red rubber balls of the era. In response and a grand display, he would fall over on the ground and lay there motionless. All our little faces would look at each other with great fear that we had just killed a priest. The circle of tiny warriors would grow smaller as we all cautiously moved closer to him, hoping he was still alive. At the very last moment, with the ring of children close around him, the black cassock would explode with a roar, and we would all scream and run away.

Father Hubert den Tandt was another young man who had just taken his vows and was training to become a Dominican Missionary to Brazil. As a kid from a 'broken home,' he was a big brother to me. He was the absolute Ying that offset the Yang I was experiencing elsewhere in the parish. I admired him in his long white Dominican robes. I enjoyed spending time with him in his yellow striped polo shirt and blue jeans. He was fun. It was always an enjoyable and relaxed time. He would take me to his parent's farm, where his mother would spread the table with the best food to ever come out of Holland. I would help him wash his car, and we would have the proverbial water fight. Initially, I waited for the other shoe to drop. I kept waiting for the 'payment due' to arrive, but it never came. He never wanted anything from me, never took from me.

He only ever gave. He was, like so many, just a decent young man who desired to serve God and humanity through the priesthood. He was good, and honest, and kind.

I will not tarnish his name, nor those of the majority, by only recalling the darkness, when so many others were light.

Chapter 8

EIN GEDI, ISRAEL AND ROAD TRIPS

It never gets old, the hour-long trip from our apartment in Bat Yam to the outskirts of Jerusalem. Bat-Yam is located on Israel's Mediterranean Sea coast and is part of the metropolitan area of Tel Aviv just south of Jaffa. In most regions of Israel, you will find public signage in Hebrew, Arabic and English. In Bat Yam, we also have Russian on most signs. Since the fall of the USSR and the collapse of the Iron Curtain, a massive influx of Russian Jews lent a unique 'Soviet Odesa / Black Sea' influence on the area. It is quite charming.

Edging east out of the city, we drop down, merging with unrestrained abandon into the honking melee of Highway 1. I hate driving in cities. The only difference in Israeli cities is the relentless volume of honking, which would embarrass even someone from Rome. The constant flash of motorcycles flying between lanes of traffic can be frightening at first. In Israel, the space between the highways' fast-moving cars is often seen and used as a motorcycle lane.

As we cross the central coastal plains, orange groves, pomegranates, all kinds of citrus farms line the road. The red flash of the bullet train blasts past you on the tracks parallel to the highway. Well-manicured homes and suburban communities reminiscent of Miami or Tampa crowd the route. Children on bikes in cul-de-sacs play Evil Knievel on little wooden ramps as their parents relax in the shade. The highway itself is perfection. It is modern, clean, well maintained and is fast-moving unless you're trying to get to Jerusalem for Purim. Then, it turns into a 95-kilometre parking lot. It is more fun and entertaining feast and a good time for the more secular residents of Tel Aviv to visit their more religious family in Jerusalem.

Winding through the Kisalon Valley, it becomes a little more forested. Small steams are momentarily visible alongside the road before they retreat into the foliage only to reappear further along. You can glimpse the terraced rocks through the trees with small herds of goats or sheep meandering the paths. It is here that the road begins to ascend. It is noticeable and it is always exciting. It always brings a sense of anticipation as you start the climb into Jerusalem. And then she's below you.

On the high ground, rising in the center of the bowl, the old city walls are glowing in the twilight.

We began our trip early enough that the lights illuminating the old city's walls are still on, and it glows golden in the mystical twilight of dawn. I smile at her as I look across, knowing her scent—the cacophony of smells, noises, and people. The shop owners will be pushing back the steel panels to display their precarious displays of spices, candies, or trinkets for the tourists. I want to stop and run in Jaffa Gate and sit at Tala, swiping my pita in the eggs and tomatoes of a hot bubbling shakshuka while sipping a robust Israeli espresso. But this is not that day.

    Today we're are just scooting around the northern part of the city and heading east to catch 90 south to Ein Gedi. A relaxing day is planned amongst the rocks and pathways, icy waterfalls and streams of the popular oasis. It is a wonderful and expansive nature reserve located just west of the Dead Sea. The sunrise gleams across the water as we slow down for a checkpoint. The Jordanian side is visible as we drive carefully into one of the lanes. A half dozen or so young armed IDF members mill around, watching as they scrutinize each vehicle. A handsome young man comes to our window, clad in green, beret on his shoulder. A few standard questions, identification, and our answers are almost all 'Ein Gedi,' and we're on our way.

    Back on the road, vast rows of date palms line the highway and remind me of driving by rows of corn in Canada. Looking across at Jordan, the haze of the heat begins to obscure the scenery. Further down the highway, I can see the red and green logo of a brightly lit Delek petrol station on the horizon. Time to stop and grab some gas, restroom break, snacks, get Sherrie a Dr. Pepper (canned in Bulgaria? Go figure). We leave the highway and weave between the ornamentally adorned camels relaxing on the sand as we park up against the building.

Sitting at the service station on the side of the interstate in Northern Michigan, I am amazed by the number of gas pumps, the neon, the flurry of human activity. My mom, sister Kerrie and I are sitting in the back seat of the little white car, and Danny O'Riley is in the front passenger seat with Father Schmid driving. We have family in Michigan, and Father Schmid supposedly has a sister in Chicago. Quite frequently, he travels to visit his sister and takes Danny with him for companionship on the trip. Occasionally we catch a ride as far as our family in Flint, where he drops us off and then picks us up upon his return a few days later. We've stopped for gas, and both my mom and Father Schmid have gone in to pay and acquire said snacks and drinks.

I didn't know Danny very well. He was 3-4 years older than me. I had served mass with him a few times, high mass usually when there was a plurality of altar boys. He got to do the incense because he was the older senior altar boy. I was a little jealous but certainly looked up to him. It wasn't much of a conversation. I don't remember much on either side of it. I remember starting a bit of a conversation in my 8-year-old way. I said something about how cool it was that he got to go to Chicago with Father Schmid. All I remember after that was Danny turning around in the passenger seat and yelling at us. His face red, his eyes bloodshot, and him raving about if I liked it, why don't I fucking go instead of him. I think it was the first time someone ever dropped the F-bomb around me. We didn't know what to do. His face protruding between the car seats, anguished eyes staring at us, Kerrie and I shrunk into our seats until his glaze retreated.

A few moments later, they returned with snacks. The car pulled away back onto the interstate. My mother told me to eat what she had given me. I sat there holding it on my lap, looking at the back of Danny's head and Father Schmid's hand on his leg. I have never forgotten that single event and still feel guilty that I didn't use all my 8-year-old powers to rescue him. Eventually, we were dropped off at Uncle Pat's house. I remember locking eyes with Danny as they pulled away. Many years later, I had heard that he had, as a man, unsuccessfully attempted suicide. I'm sorry Danny, I failed you back then.

The jingle of the bells on the saddles of the camels pulls me back to the present. Once again, my history had hijacked my today. A couple of these big, beautifully ugly 'ships of the desert' are passing my driver's side window as I sit in the parking lot. The warm Negev Desert air is stifling. Sherrie is already in the Delek station. I need to think of why I took so long to follow her inside.

Chapter 9

TOMBSTONE, ARIZONA AND THE BLUE CHAIRS

Wherever I've lived, I've always made an effort to know the history of the place. Growing up in Woodstock, I hung out a lot at the museum in the city square. The curator at the time, Mr. Milnes, would always be there to answer my questions and to point out items of interest along with their story. In San Angelo, Texas, I appreciated the city more because I learned of its origins with Fort Concho and the Buffalo Soldiers.

In the mid-1980s, I was stationed in Mainz, West Germany, with the US 8th Infantry Division, where I was quartered at Robert E. Lee Barracks in Gonsenheim. Heading out on training, we would often blast up the Rhine River barely over the water in a wolf pack of 4 Blackhawk helicopters.

Both sides of the mighty river presented a constant view of castles in various states of use and abandonment. Occasionally the pilot would break away and slowly hover down into the center of an abandoned stone castle courtyard. I was in my glory. I never understood the troops stationed in Germany, who would live on base, shop at the commissary, go to the movie theatre on base, shop at the PX on base, and patronize the various bars on base. They might as well be posted to Cleveland or somewhere for all the culture or world experience they were gaining.

In Kabul, I spent what little downtime I had by reading the history of the place. Of Ghengis Khan and the Mongolian hordes swarming down into the city. Of the British in Kyber Pass and the 1842 retreat from Kabul, the Massacre of Elphinstone's army, during the First Anglo-Afghan War and the more recent stories of the warrior Massoud. I had the opportunity to spend days with the Mongolians who were part of the coalition forces and ride along in their convoys. I remember having difficulty keeping a grin off my face when I rode over the ridge and headed down into Kabul with the Mongolians! I was able to appreciate the historical significance as we passed remnants of the original stone walls built by Tamerlane.

Sherrie and I taught at a small private elementary school in the early 80s. With only a couple dozen students ranging from grade 4 to grade 8, it was sometimes challenging to find activities to supplement the wide range of curricula. The occasional field trip offered an opportunity for exploration at all ages and levels. Being a history junkie, I decided to take the kids an hour away to Tombstone.

Tombstone is an iconic cowboy town with a unique and questionable history. You can't think of Tombstone without thinking of Wyatt Earp, Virgil and Morgan, the OK Corral with Doc Holiday, the Clantons and the McLaurys. It is of interest to all ages and provides a great starting point for discussions of morality, ethics, and humanity.

The town has retained most of its historic flavour without becoming Vegas, Niagara Falls or Gatlingburg. Many historic silver-boom era buildings still stand, such as the Bird Cage Theater, Schieffelin Hall, and the courthouse. Much of the main street is period buildings housing museums dedicated to various aspects of the area's history. The Gunfighter Hall of Fame, despite its name, held one of the most complete and well documented collections on a wide variety of local history. We lined the kids up for the introduction, and we received a welcome from our tour guide who was a grisly but charming elder gentleman who looked like he might have personally known Wyatt Earp.

As we funneled the kids into the museum, the air conditioning was a welcome relief from the 102 degrees Arizona morning. Little eyes were open wide as the guide described the wonders within. As I acclimated from the bright sun outside, I observed a second distinguished gentleman sitting behind one of the display counters. He had his chair tilted back with his cowboy hat cocked down, almost touching his Sam Elliot stache. The chair was a little out of place with its 60's bent tube frame and turquoise Naugahyde covering.

I don't know how long he had been there, and I only know that I woke up because his hands were touching me. My bedroom was dark, but the light from the hallway cast into the room and illuminated the turquoise blue Naugahyde-covered chair from the kitchen. My mother had crazy 1960's tastes because our kitchen counters were the same gaudy shade of blue.

I lay there immobilized by my fear, confusion, and the fact that I was still semi-awake. The hands continued to explore me as I squinted through slightly opened eyes. It was a man in black, but it was definitely not Johnny Cash. The chair was from our kitchen, and it wasn't here in my room when I went to bed.

I could hear animated voices coming from the living room. I recognized my moms' voice but not the other, and maybe a third. It wasn't my father as they were separated again for another short forever. I was cold and wanted to pull the covers and my pajamas back up, but any movement might betray that I was awake. I lay there wondering how it was possible that this person had come into my house and had carried a chair from the kitchen to my bedroom. How had he disappeared into my room without my mom or the other people noticing. I prayed they would soon notice the missing chair and would rush to remove it, and him, from my frozen nightmare.

It never happened. The cheerful voices and laughter continued. Amazing the things that can go through my eight-year-old mind as the air in my room grew stiller and darker and wetter. The juvenile acceptance that this was ordained and that I was the problem, permeated the external, and internal darkness.

Eventually, the covers were casually tossed back on me as the black figure left my room. As he walked through my doorframe, it was hard for me to tell the man from the shadow. I remember that his presence blocked light as he left. When I was sure he was gone, I pulled my pajamas back on and moved to the far side of the bed, where I befriended the safety of the wall. In the morning, the chair was still in my room, and there were numerous Black Label and Red Cap bottles in the living room.

Even here, over forty years later, in a happy time on a sunny day, the grimy shadowy fingers of the past reach out to touch me again.

Chapter 10

BATTLE OF SHILO, TENNESSEE AND SHATTERED STUDIES

The giant red paddlewheel on the back of the steamboat methodically thumped on impact as each massive wooden board hit the clear water of the Tennessee River. I loved the Tennessee River as it provided a much more intimate journey than the other rivers on which I spent so much of my time. It was cleaner and clearer also. You could tell the difference. Coming up the Mississippi from the deep south, you would begin to see a slight colour change in the water on each bank. The closer you got to Cairo Point, the more pronounced it became. The west side of the river was muddy brown, while the eastern side of the river was a deeper, darker shade. The Ohio River flowed into the mighty and muddy Mississippi on the east side. Steering to starboard, we would watch the big muddy disappear behind the trees and the great Ohio laid out in a bright ribbon before us.

Today our time on the Ohio would be limited. Once again, we notice the river distinctively divided by the colour of the water. As we approach Paducah, Kentucky, on high ground to the right, with its flood walls and massive steel flood gates, the confluence of the Tennessee River becomes remarkable. The Ohio now appears the muddy one as it has flowed from Pittsburgh and carries much more silt and other material. The Tennessee, which winds through its namesake state, Alabama, and ultimately ends here in Kentucky, is a much clearer river. The clearness is partly due to the harder rock bottom and solid valleys it has travelled through.

Shortly we will begin our crossing of the Kentucky Lakes, the only real open water on our trip. A little more precarious crossing for a flat-bottom boat, where notice of the weather and waves demand closer attention. After a few hours of steaming, we pass Nathan Bedford Forrest State Park on the right and pass under the New Johnsonville bridge. Soon we will be back on the river where we belong.

The Tennessee River becomes relatively narrow at many points, and you could call out to people onshore. Moderate wooden homes and fishing shacks line the banks, and apart from the occasional rusty beer fridge, you could convince yourself into thinking that you have travelled back a century or more.

My favourite time of the day was the early morning before the passengers were up and noisy. I would take my coffee and stand alone on the very point of the bow of the boat.

It was only a few feet above the water as a flat bottom steamboat has very little freeboard. There would be a haze of mist rolling gently on most summer mornings. Sometimes it was thick enough that I couldn't even see the river, just me with my coffee slowly and gently gliding through the clouds around me. As the early morning warmed, the mist would rise, and if you dropped to one knee, you could see up river with the clouds slowly swirling just above your head. It was a fresh sweet southern pine-scented mist that laid as a canopy over everything. Splashing on the starboard side and I meet the eyes of a young wet deer looking at me as it frantically swims for shore. I lower my head, and as we pass gently by, I see it lunge up onto the banks and disappear up into the fog. A few more hours, and we would come alongside in Savannah, Tennessee.

Mr. Croxford was the principal of St. Michael's Elementary School in Woodstock for the entirety of my time there. He was a rock, a disciplinarian, and a caring, concerned, and thoughtful leader. He also had a passion for the American Civil War. In grade 6, 7 and 8 history classes, I learned more about the Battle of Gettysburg, Antietam, Chickamauga, the Seige of Vicksburg, Shiloh, and men like Robert E Lee, Ulysses Grant than I ever learned about The Plains of Abraham or Wolf and Montcalm. Mr. Croxford had lit a flame in me so that I also had a passion for the history of the civil war. Shortly we would be landing across the river from Shiloh National Military Park, which preserves the battlefield of the Battle of Shiloh.

As we rounded the bend in the river, you could begin to pick up the scent of campfires under the pines. As the boat maneuvered towards the riverbank, various swatches of pastel colours began to appear onshore. From a distance it began to look like the Royal Doulton shelf in my grandmothers' parlour. And there they were, stepping out to the edge of the river, about a dozen southern belles in flowing antebellum dresses, accompanied by uniformed soldiers of the old south. All of them waving, all of them here to welcome the riverboat. The whistles would blow and the giant steam calliope on the top deck would begin to play Dixie. Here, in the land of cotton, old times here are definitely not forgotten.

Mr. Croxford had talked to my mother when I was in grade six. He had shared his opinion that he viewed me as someone with reasonably adept academic potential. He had requested her permission to issue me some curriculum from University of Western Ontario history courses, and she agreed. A week or two later, I was proud as I slogged home the enormous and heavy textbook. My assignment was to begin reading the chapters and answering in paragraph form the questions at the end of each chapter. I could do that.

That evening I sat on one of the blue chairs at the kitchen table. I slowly opened the hard, shiny textbook's cover with almost religious reverence. Finding chapter one, I began to read. I have no memory of the era of history I was studying. After finishing the chapter, I read the questions. Question 1, I wrote a small #1 in pencil in the 'scribbler' he had provided. I carefully wrote my answer. And then question 2. Again, I thought back on what I had just read and wrote down my response. I was somewhat surprised that this was what university studies entailed as I looked back to read question 3.

    Engrossed in my' studies,' I hadn't noticed the melee beginning in the far corner of the kitchen. The dishes getting knocked to the floor and shattering also shattered my concentration. Locked in a violent struggle, my parents were again in a physical confrontation. The screaming began. I was somewhat immune to the content of the screaming as my father broke free of the struggle and walked past me. At the same time, a pot of hot water hit the wallpaper behind me, aimed at him. He screamed and turned around. My sister entered the room crying. In the flurry of actions and screaming, I heard the phrase "fucking priests." Figurative or literal, who was to say. My mother launched a second projectile, this one smashing the ceiling lights and bulbs over the table where I sat. The room fell dark. I crunched across the broken glass in my bare feet, and Kerrie took me to hide together in her room.

    I never worked on the UWO study again. I really can't explain why. I remember Mr. Croxford's look of disappointment when I returned the textbook. I've wondered what might have been if I had been able to pursue the path he had considered for me.

Chapter 11

DUBAI, UNITED ARAB EMIRATES AND WATTER

Every military in the world is heavy on acronyms, and the Canadian Armed Forces is no different. It almost becomes a dialect of its own that any civilian would be challenged to understand. Most deployed service members' favourite acronym is HLTA – Home Leave Travel Assistance.

HLTA, by simplest definition, is travel leave for members deployed over six months. The intent is to cover the cost during those six months for the member to reunite with their immediate next of kin back home. If they send you away from your family for six months, they will pay for you to come home and visit for two weeks during that period.

My HLTA from Afghanistan was a welcome respite from the heat, dirt, and mostly the stress of living 24/7 in the presence of an armed enemy set on your destruction. The simple method of getting out of the country was a series of hoops and ladders. For individual leave such as HLTA, you are booked on a civilian airline. You cannot fly on a civilian airline in full combat gear or, advisably, any clothing which would identify you as a military member. Therefore, as you are initially packing for deployment, you must bring one pair of civilian clothes. It made sense now. You also must travel to the airport from wherever you are stationed in-country. You also must be ready, should the waste material hit the air circulator, to return fire and engage the enemy on the way to the airport.

So, when the escort convoy of armoured SUVs shows up to transport your ass, you must be out there in your civilian clothing, with helmet, full tac-vest with plates, long weapon and sidearm. All in all, I felt pretty goofy in my civi's, ready for a 28-hour series of flights, while sporting full arid-cadpat battle rattle. I tossed my suitcase in the vehicle and hopped in.

The drive through Kabul was its usual uneventful series of events. Soviet-era destroyed buildings, beautiful new glass wedding halls, goats, sheep, horses, trucks loaded with armed men glaring at the convoy, the usual. Driving through the gateway to the KIA - Kabul International Airport (future notoriety unknown at the time), the grounds were almost park-like. Trees, green grass, a few degrees cooler, or so it seemed because of the greenery. This time we rolled up to the civilian side of the long blue terminal. The main entrance is open to pedestrian traffic. The traffic lane in front is blocked with considerable concrete barriers to prevent the bad guys from detonating a vehicle nearby.

The SUVs stop. I replace my helmet with a ball cap, drop my tac vest and gear and pass my C7 and 9mm to an escorting corporal from the Van Doos. We both signed the sheet with the serial numbers as all of these items will greet me upon my return in two weeks. I grab my small carry-on full of pashminas and other trinkets for the folks back home and head, feeling quite naked, across the asphalt to the terminal. The big white and blue Safi Airlines waits in the distance. First stop, Dubai.

It is twilight as we bank low over the Persian Gulf and make our final approach into Dubai. It is breathtaking. After the last few months in a tungsten-lit sandbox, the carpet of illumination lays out like only Aladdin or Disney could imagine. A giant glistening palm tree-shaped suburb, built into the water, twinkles as I see vehicles moving along its modern streets. We touch down in what comparatively seems like Vegas from the Safi window. The next flight is in 8 hours, a Lufthansa to Frankfurt.

Once in the airport, I was unsure which was to go. I feel vulnerable without my combat gear, and my sneakers feel like when you take those first few steps after taking off your ice skates. I follow the flow of humanity into a large reception area. Along one wall are about 20 customs booths with a gentleman in brilliant white dishdasha and headdress operating each station. Emanating from each one is a line of people holding their passports. As at Cosco, I choose my line.

Standing in queue, slowly kicking my carry-on ahead of me with each step, I notice the guy behind me seems to be just as much out of place as I am. I strike up a conversation with him and find he's also a Canadian army sergeant stationed at Camp Phoenix in Kabul, also heading on HLTA. We chat for the 20 minutes it takes us to get to the front of the line. It's my turn. The dignified-looking younger man behind the glass motions me forward. He looks at my passport and asks how long I intend to be in the United Arab Emirates. I tell him I am just passing through on my way to Canada. He hands my passport back and informs me I don't need to be in this line, that I should have turned right into the airport terminal, not left. I sheepishly take my passport and motion the sarge to follow me.

Turning right instead, we entered the lavish Dubai airport. Standing on the people mover slowly gliding between rows of 100-foot palm trees, I see Starbucks and gold bullion vending machines, restaurants, and bars. Having been in a no alcohol environment for months, I suggested to the good sergeant that we might perhaps partake of an alcoholic beverage. He politely nods his acquiescence to my proposal.

Entering the lounge, we grabbed a couple of the comfy chairs with the small coffee table between them and settled in. It was weird being back on earth and a world away, from a world away. As the pretty little server came over, I looked over at the taps and ordered the first round for us. Navy takes the lead over Army with an opening bid of 3 pints each of Carlsberg at $18 each, my buy.

The coffee table in the front living room of St. Rita's rectory is a rigid wooden rectangle, even slightly outdated for the era. The curtains are heavy, blocking out the lights and sounds of Dundas Street outside. The ashtray on the table has eight or ten Carlsberg beer caps in it, and they are jingling together as the coffee table moves back and forth rythmically. I am looking down from directly over the ashtray, watching the caps, and the table is warm against my abdomen. The taste of the beer is in my mouth, and I'm contemplating why the bottles are a weird shape from the usual Red Cap or Black Label stubbies.

And that's it. I've tried to expand that memory. I know I was older than my time with Fr. Schmid. I remember sitting on the sofa holding the weird-shaped bottle. I remember Fr. Watter seated in the chair to the right. I remember watching the bottle caps dancing in the ashtray. Every time I concentrate and try to see more, and a hint appears in my peripheral vision, I turn my head to see, and it's gone. What is always perceivable, though, over the past 40 plus years, is the sick feeling I have in the pit of my stomach whenever I see the Carlsberg logo. That ill feeling invariably is accompanied by the vision of the ashtray.

Not too much later, I learned that Fr. Watter was in the hospital in Stratford. Kerrie drove, and we went to see him.

What was once a large, exuberant, energetic man was now a hollow skeleton, frail in the sheets of the hospital bed. We tried to visit with him and make conversation, but he would have none of it. He was distraught and inconsolable. He was moaning loudly, groaning, deeply disturbing wailing from the pit of his soul. "I'm going to hell, the things I have done" were the only words he would say, "I'm going to hell." We left him there and could still hear him as we walked the hallway to the elevator.

Once back in the car we sat for a while in silence. Kerrie said nothing. I sat thinking of all the Carlsberg caps in the ashtray.

Six Carlsberg, that's $108 US dollars said our server as she placed three pints each in front of the good sergeant and me. I added a tip and swiped my card. We both picked up our first beer in months and toasted HLTA. It was cold, crisp, almost hurt, and was so good. The sarge got the second round and then we alternated back and after that. I like Carlsberg, it's a fine beer. I have wondered over the years though, how many Carlsberg would I have to drink to forget the Carlsberg?

Chapter 12

THE BERLIN WALL
AND TAMPONS

It felt strange having a priest in my home after all these years. The last time I saw the black clothing with a clerical collar in my house, it was a completely different situation, and I was a lifetime younger.

The concrete towers along the zone protruded from the landscape like white pegs in a cribbage board. There was always at least one visible, and usually more as they rosaried their way along the East German or the 'Deutsche Demokratische Republik' (DDR) border. My US Army jeep convoy snaked its way along the trail, which ran beside the massive fence on our side of the deforested strip of 'no man's land between the two countries. My breakfast was filling, my jacket was warm, and Ronal Regan was president. All was good.

Not much ever really happened. We would drive our section and turn and drive back. It was a presence patrol to reinforce to The East that we were here; we watched them and they watched us. Occasionally we would stop and get out to stretch. We would look through our high-powered binoculars at the DDR guards in their towers, watching us. I would salute them with my middle finger and in the round shimmering view in the bino's, I would see one of them 'salute' me back. It was a basic standard operating procedure.

Sporadically I would read in Stars and Stripes newspaper about an individual or family who had escaped the DDR somewhere along the border and made it to The West. It was always fascinating reading of unimaginable bravery and chance. I developed an interest in the East and would take the troop train from Helmstedt across east Germany into West Berlin. The passenger rail usually ran at night and neither stopped nor slowed down until it came into the large, fenced compound at the border. When the train lurched to a stop, I would watch the DDR border police file onto the platform. Their leather jackets and sharply peaked caps were still eerily reminiscent of imagery of the SS in the Nazi era. Their gloved hands held a chain attached to a large German Sheppard completed the visuals. In the amber glow of the platform lights, they would slowly and methodically inspect the train. One guard would push a hand trolly with a large mirror facing upwards, while another guard would shine a bright spotlight on the mirror. It would reflect up onto the train car's undercarriage, inspecting that no one was clinging under in the hope of escape. The dogs, with their muscular haunches and intimidating jowls, patrolled alongside. The guards were not allowed on the train, so the gates would open after all external inspections had been completed. We would lurch forward, screeching and rolling into the west. It was good to see neon, colour, lights and even McDonalds once again.

I had left the US Army by the time the wall came down. I was glued to the television, watching an icon I had known well, and despised, being pulled down by the very people it had separated. I watched the dominos of Eastern European counties fall, and the Union of Soviet Socialist Republics collapse. I wanted to be there. I wanted to be part of it.

One night, watching CNN, they interviewed a young family in Russia. They asked questions like How was this new freedom going? How did they feel about the transition to a free-market economy? The young father whom they featured was despondent. Because of the new 'freedoms,' his factory had closed, and he was out of a job. He had a wife and three children, which the camera panned over to. They were about the same age as my children and they were eating an almost transparent broth, and the mom wasn't eating. The father opened a small wooden cupboard and showed the meagre foodstuffs they had, with limited options to replenish those. I wanted to help.

As I watched, I thought that I would be glad to help if I could help that specific family and send them boxes of food.

I wasn't someone who aspired to donate to large humanitarian organizations, with perceived colossal overhead and trickle-down assistance. But, if I could help THAT family, I would. Over the next few days, I replayed the CNN story in my head. I saw the children's faces. I heard the heartbreak in their fathers' voice, and it all churned in my soul. If this was democracy, why would they want it? In time no doubt, the system would settle, but in the interim, they needed assistance. As I contemplated options, simplicity reared its uncommon head. If I would help a specific family with boxes of food, vitamins, whatever, then other Canadians would no doubt be willing to do the same. I pitched the idea to Sherrie and a good friend. With nothing to lose, a few friends and I headed to Ottawa.

On a wing and a prayer, we rang the buzzer on the fenced gate at the Russian Embassy. A thickly accented voice inquired as to our purpose. I briefly tried to explain, but halfway through my rambling, the buzzer sounded, and the gate opened. As we walked the sidewalk up to the very Stalinist architecture building, a gentleman came out to greet us. Oleg Krokhalev would become a good friend and fellow traveler over the next few years. Inside the embassy, we sat in a small parlour and explained our desire and plan to Oleg. If he could provide the names and addresses of genuinely needy families, we would do everything we could to find a Canadian family to assist them. Our program would be called 'Family to Family.' He smiled and seemed to like the idea. He shook our hands and told us he'd see what he could do as he ushered us back out the gate.

We were in Ottawa, and embassies were everywhere. Our experience with the Russians seemed to go reasonably well. Let's maximize our time here. The large Victorian-era home had the flag of Bulgaria hanging from the porch as we knocked on their door. Mrs. Kolev, the wife of the Bulgarian Charge d'affairs, ushered us in through the kitchen. Her husband joined us in the living room as we all sat on folding chairs. They were new to Canada by only a few weeks. As I began to explain our idea, she motioned with her hand to speak quieter. She explained that the other people moving boxes and such around were the old communist staff packing to leave. Once again, the Family-to-Family idea of connecting caring Canadians with needy Bulgarians was accepted and appreciated with the same 'we'll see what we can do' response.

On we went to the Romanian Embassy, and once again, we were knocking on the door with no appointment. The outcome was the same. There was nowhere else to go, so we went for lunch. There was not yet a Ukrainian, Latvian, Lithuanian or other independent former Soviet embassy in Ottawa. So, we headed home. Did we accomplish anything? We didn't know. We would wait and see.

A week went by, two weeks, almost three weeks and nothing. And then, near the end of the third week, I opened the mailbox, and there was a single letter with a Bulgarian postmark. The young couple and their children in Stara Zagora, Bulgaria, said they had heard about our program, desperately needed help, and would love to be matched with a Canadian family. We all sat at my kitchen table with teary eyes, passing the letter back and forth, reading and re-reading it. We would help this family.

The next day I could hardly contain my excitement as I went to the post office to check the mail. When I opened the box, my heart dropped with disappointment as there was no mail, just a white card. The card said to see the lady at the counter. She gave me an odd look when I handed her the card. She returned with three white mail sacks containing just over 1600 pieces of mail.

Where do we begin? We once again sat at my kitchen table, pulling a handful of letters at a time. We would open one and cry, then open another and cry again. Most of the stamps had some version of Lenin on them. They were from Russia, Bulgaria, Romania, Moldova, Ukraine, Latvia, and more. Some included newspaper clippings from the Nevsky Times containing articles about us and our address. Others said they heard about Family-to-Family on broadcasts from Radio Baltica, Radio Liberty, Radio Canada International, and more. Others said they were informed of Family to Family program by Anatoli Sobchak's office as the Mayor of St. Petersburg, the same from the office of Valerie Pop, Mayor of Moscow. Some included photos, little printed religious icons, and other precious trinkets. We bought laundry baskets and began to sort mail into one-child, two-child, teacher, single mother, nurse, etc., categories along the floor in my basement. And the letters kept coming. The Canadian Security Intelligence Service showed up on our doorstep at one point. The amount of 'soviet' mail coming through Montreal's main international postal sorting facility had alerted them.

Now to generate a Canadian response. Local London TV and newspapers did a story which other news organizations picked up. Hundreds responded locally and were matched. Requests came in from Toronto, Calgary, Vancouver, and all across Canada asking if they could participate. People would write and ask if their sister in New Zealand could also help a family, and we would twin them and then inform their local New Zealand newspaper for follow-up. Their story would now empower us to match hundreds of Kiwi families. We continued to work with the embassies, adding new embassies and expanding our reach. We continued to push feel-good stories to media in the local areas of all the western families participating. All this was in the early pre-internet 1990s.

Over time, and with information from initial requests combined with feedback from host families, we assembled a suggested list of items to send. Anything perishable was naturally not included, and anything in glass jars was also not recommended. Children's multi-vitamins were high on the list, lightweight items like flavoured pasta, dry beans, tea and coffee, soup mixes, etc. Also, we had an increased request for feminine hygiene products. I remember my wife opening and reading one letter from Russia in which the young mother requested tampons. She explained how tiring and frustrating it was every month to sit at her grandmothers old foot pedal machine, with cotton and fabric and string and tightly roll and sew tampons or pads for herself.

In the end, as the world changed and situations stabilized, we had ultimately twinned over 8,000 families in 38 countries. We loved to hear and promote the stories of families we assisted in helping. Children of poorer eastern families attended university and staying with their western families. There were weddings (though we weren't a dating agency, some successful romances did occur). And numerous visits paid for by Canadian and US families bringing their eastern families for a visit. There were even some stories of immigration sponsorship and assistance.

We worked with various churches, organizations, social groups, teachers' unions, etc. So, when Father 'Wally' from the local Roman Catholic Church came to my basement office, it was not unexpected. My buddy and wife and I gave him a little tour of the one-room basement still loaded with thousands of letters, maps with pins, stamps, and a wall of newspaper articles from around the globe.

His visit was a good one. He was a good guy. He would occasionally reappear with sincere words of encouragement and prayers for continued success. I accepted invitations to speak to groups at the church. Amid everything we had accomplished, I still sat staring at his clerical collar and as much as I tried, as irrelevant as he was to my intimate history, I couldn't get rid of the knot in my stomach.

Chapter 13

THE GREEN BEAN AND A SMALL STEP

The Green Bean Coffee Company was a lifesaver. Down south in Kandahar, they had a Tim Hortons on base. Here in Kabul, at Camp Eggers, we had a Green Bean. Working 18–20-hour days, seven days a week, coffee was an essential part of life. Various times during the day, if we were inside the wire, I would feel my energy level draining and the heavy blanket of fatigue covering me. It was in this fog that a fellow camouflage-clad colleague would say 'Green Bean?'. Hell yes, was invariably my response.

Green Bean was a small coffee company based in California with the catchphrase' Honour First, Coffee Second'. They specialized in providing excellent coffee and the 'boutique café experience' on military bases, even in active conflict zones. They also had an online program called 'Cup of Joe for a Joe' where anyone could buy a random deployed member their next cup of coffee and include a personal message. The bean here on Eggers was heaven-sent.

It was housed in a modified shipping container, like almost everything on base. A small wooden extension provided a bit of shade. The sliding door led into a small airconditioned sanctuary with the heavy scent of roasting beans and the magic juggling show of the Afghan baristas preparing hot joe and creamy chai. The lineup waiting was a camo-quilt of assorted patterns from around the world. Thirty-four different designs, from Canadian arid CADPAT to Romanian mosaic, to what we jokingly called the Australian Clown Pajamas, were all represented.

The shipping container sat on a little broken-stone plaza containing a few ancient grape vines and gnarled tree stubs still clinging to life. In pre-Soviet pre-Taliban times, this area had been an upscale neighbourhood with homes of foreign ambassadors and some of Afghanistan's elite. Today the base utilized the few remaining houses and grounds within the camp's walls. The area's history was never as evident as one evening when we loaded boxes of foreign donated children's shoes down into a temporary underground storage unit. I was confused about why the walls were blue until the sergeant pointed out that it was, in fact, a former swimming pool. Life is strange.

The temperature was in the high 30 Celsius today. There was a slight welcome breeze that was equally hot but circulated the air a bit. The ad-hoc collection of rusty, paint-peeling, metal patio tables and chairs looked like an explosion in your grandparents' backyard in 1968. I balanced our two coffees as not to slosh the contents through the hole in the plastic lid. We had sat in the two chairs at the small table against the gabion basket wall. His boyish face lit up with a genuinely handsome smile as I said I'd grab us each a coffee. As I walked back across the stones, I noticed the troops at the other tables going about their business, chatting, planning, whatever. Others were walking by his table, unaware.

He looked up as I placed his coffee on the rusty table. As I pulled my chair out and sat across from him, my combat boot inadvertently kicked his foot. I couldn't help but think how I had just kicked the foot that took 'one small step for man.' And there we sat. Neil Armstrong and I, chatting and sipping our coffee. He seemed genuinely interested in my job and experience within the country. He was a total gentleman, military brother, professional, and absolute class act.

My mom spread a couple of blankets on the floor in the living room. My older sister and I carried our pillows out from the bedroom and placed them on the floor. The old black plastic Admiral television, rabbit ears extended fully, flickered in the corner. It was a warm July night in 1969, and air conditioning had not yet reached our minor planet. We got comfortable on the palate on the rug. The glow from the television illuminated the blueish fog from my mom's incessant chain-smoking, broken only by the momentary blaze and sizzle of the next cigarette being lit. She loved space and anything to do with it. Maybe because her life here was such refuse that she took mental refuge in things so otherworldly, she loved it, and she did pass that on to my sister and me. We were always allowed to stay home from school and join her in watching any launch from Cape Kennedy. Sometimes she didn't even make us go to school when the launch was over. We truly also loved space.

"Quit picking at your butt," my mom barked from somewhere in the nicotine cloud behind me. The austere monotone voice on the television was narrating the events. I cared. I was young, but I was aware that I was watching history in the making. I wanted to see this. "Quit squirming around," she again barked, this time with a boney-toe prod to the back of the head. I tried to lay still. I pulled the blanket up to my chin with the hope it would cloak my movements.

The evening mass was over. I preferred to serve Mass on a Sunday night, as it meant I could sleep in or play longer on a Sunday morning. Night mass was always shorter and more effortless than morning or high Mass. All I could think of was the moon landing later tonight as I walked off the altar. Late. We would go to bed at our regular time, but then my mother would wake us up sometime in the darkness so that we could witness man's first step on the moon. I quickly removed my cassock and cleaned the cruets from the water and wine, leaving them upside-down on a paper towel to air dry. I turned to get my jacket, and he was there.

There would be no clean getaway tonight.

A few steps down from the sacristy, there was a small bathroom. On the right was the tiny room with a toilet and sink. On the left was the crash bar of the heavy exit door. His hand was on my shoulder as we walked down the few steps. I stared at the exit door and drastically wanted to bolt, but his hand was heavy on me. The bathroom door closed behind us, I heard the lock click, and I instinctively turned and held both sides of the small sink jutting out from the wall. The white porcelain was cold. In the polished taps, I could see the distorted reflection of both of us—the pink of me, shadowed by the giant black reflection of him behind me.

I gripped the sink and wondered what the moon would be like. Would it swallow the astronauts when they stepped on it? Would they be sucked into it? Would a hole appear and aliens attack? For a moment, I returned from space and realized my duties were not yet over. His hands were still on me, moving, exploring, probing. This time was different. This was much bigger than his fingers. I held the sink tighter as I could feel my feet lifted off the floor. How did astronauts eat? I had heard something about them having ice cream, and I imagined it would be nice to have ice cream in the darkness of space.

I laid as still as possible as not to annoy my mother. My hand was secretively under the blanket attending to my ache. I would pray later for forgiveness. Right now, in the eerie flickering glow of the televised moonscape, white legs and boots were coming down the ladder. His boot touched the sand of the moon, and nothing happened. And then the other foot. No aliens, no attacks, no one swallowed up. In the silver darkness of that 1969 night, a voice said, "One small step for man, one giant leap for mankind." I heard my mom sniff, and over my shoulder, I could see the glisten of the tears on her cheeks.

Holding his paper Green Bean cup, Neil Armstrong was staring at me. He had said something and was waiting for my response. I had no idea what he had said. The twisted maelstrom of my past had again blasted into my present and left a momentary trail of destruction. I said 'sorry,' and he graciously repeated his question. He found it amusing that here in Afghanistan, we sometimes joked about when we got home, calling it 'when we get back on earth.' Not quite the literal meaning it had for him. He chuckled. For an all too short amount of time, we continued our conversation. We had a few laughs and relaxed for a short time. I saw his gaze raise above me. I saw his friends coming to gather him up, looking over my shoulder. Neil Armstrong introduced me to Jim Lovell and Gene Cernan as I stood up.

And then they left. I stood silently, and with every ounce of my being, I watched, intent on imprinting this memory in my mind forever. The three heroes in matching white shirts and tan pants walked away. They were chatting and chuckling like only those whose lifetime bonded them as brothers could understand.

    Within a year, US Navy Lieutenant Armstrong would pass.

    Twice he had entered my life. The moon landing had for a lifetime been instinctively bound to dread, sadness, and pain. That day, in the 20 minutes I was privileged to have his company, he unknowingly replaced those memories. With his humble kindness, compassion and genuine boyish smile and laughter, his presence healed at least one wound. For a moment, I walked with a giant.

Chapter 14

YORKVILLE VILLAGE, TORONTO, AND THE RETURN OF CEILING TILES

The men tended to be cleaner than the women.

Men tended to leave the house with the intention of finding you. Finding someone to fill in the blanks, empty spaces, and heart-voids temporarily remedied through the tender, though purchased salve of intimate human contact. They prepped, cleaned, trimmed, and fussed like they would be on display for personal approval. Most were shy, and most were lonely. Most really wanted acceptance and wanted to connect more than just physically. Though they all still wanted the physical.

Women were different. They didn't prep, and they didn't care. Ownership was more important to them, even if it was just for 30 or 60 minutes, and you'd take what you were given. It was the mid 70's, and drinking and driving were, unfortunately, more commonplace. Yorkville Village in Toronto was re-immerging from its Bohemian, counterculture, patchouli identity of the '60s into a trendier upscale coffee shop era of the mid-'70s. The cool people hung out in Yorkville. The fashionable, the stylish, the swank. It was a place to see and be seen. It was a place for those with money to buy what they wanted and those without money to sell what they had. It was a no-questions-asked island of access in the city for every type of suburban decadence.

The decision to pull up at the curb in Yorkville was usually inspired by the 5th Cosmo and a husband who had to 'work late.' For the most part, they weren't even nice. There was always a parking garage, lot, or dark alley nearby. They requisitioned the mechanics of what you had to offer and demanded their money's worth. Most never got it. But only because of their confessed inability to arrive after the volume of cocktails they had consumed. And that was fine. There was only a limited financial stimulus per vehicle, so the more cars you could move along, the better.

Men were sad. Women were angry.

As a rule, we preferred the women even though they were not as plentiful. It had nothing to do with sexuality, orientation, or genitalia. It all had to do with mathematics. Quite simply, the number of times you can perform a requested task, the more money ends up in your pocket. Men predominantly wanted to do various things to you; women wanted you to do something to them. With a woman, you could play-act, improvise, you could fake it, and not one of them ever cared enough to notice; with a man, it was almost impossible. They needed the evidence. You could be back on the street quickly and productively after being with a woman. In contrast, it usually required more recovery time after you were with a man.

You could always make some initial evaluations as you approached the car. Although this was never an accurate indicator, the obvious items such as how expensive the vehicle was, affluent people often held their money with a much tighter fist than the average working person who needed to blow off steam. Another evaluation was whether the car license plate had a rental frame. Again though, this was never a valid indicator to judge business negotiations by, but it helped. People travelling for business were often away from their moral compasses, church, spouse, friends that would keep them from exploring at home. They were usually more willing to part with their coin and less sure of what they wanted or how to ask for it. You could lead them along much more effortlessly.

Leaning in the car window, you had to make immediate judgement calls. If the car was filthy, the driver probably was also. And no matter how hungry you were, sometimes that could be a dealbreaker. Was there heavy drug paraphernalia? If so, it was usually a showstopper for me. Was there a third person in the car? Sometimes that made a difference, certainly in price.

Occasionally someone would approach you on foot—usually, a guest staying nearby at the Four Seasons or Hilton on Yonge. Once the negotiations were completed, you would have to accompany your new owner back to their room. I hated the lobby. The hotel employees eventually recognized you, and their eyes would watch you accompany their oblivious guest across the hall to the elevator. There wasn't a single time I made that walk that I didn't think of the disapproving glare of housekeeper Bessie at St. Rita's. It was appropriate that my mind would always return there, as it was there I did my apprenticeship, where I learned my trade.

At some point, a little later in life, I understood that staring at the ceiling tile could pay more than pocket-change or a candy bar. There is a skill to staring at ceiling tiles. Altogether remove yourself from the situation and only occasionally mentally return if only to check on the status of the person occupying your space, or to look at your watch. Looking around the room was easier because of the weird abstract 70's art that even quality hotels of the time had. I remember thinking it was easier in the hotel than in the rectory. Here in the hotel, I didn't have to try to avoid the omnipresent disapproving gaze of the crucified figure on the wall.

At the end of one prosperous weekend, I crashed again on the sofa of a friend who was an exotic dancer on Yonge St at Zanzibar. A beautiful little Asian girl named Tisha. Her story had some of the same hallmarks as mine, and often we would lay side-by-side and envision what future we each might find. When the sun rose, we would stumble out into the pre-Starbucks era morning searching for a decent coffee.

One morning we ended up at The Bay on Yonge, where I bought a pair of soft calfskin pants costing over $300. Why? I'm not sure. I guess I just liked them. It was a teen in the '70s.

Chapter 15

BALLAST AND BARNACLES

Ballast [bal-uhst]
noun
- *a heavy substance placed in such a way as to improve stability and control*
- *anything that gives mental, moral, or political stability or steadiness:*
verb
- *to ballast a ship.*
- *to give steadiness to; keep steady*

Think of ballast as balance. It helps to keep the vessel centered and upright in the water. The higher a ship sits in the water, the top-heavier it is and easier it would be to capsize. Loading ballast increases the ship's weight and pulls it lower into the water. Any boat must balance the weight above the waterline with weight below the centerline.

Too little make the vessel easier to capsize, too much and the ship sits too low in the water and is slower to respond. It's all about the center of mass being slightly below the waterline. It is the ballast that provides stability.

I would not wish my experiences on anyone, and I would go to extreme personal measures to rescue any young child held hostage in this situation. I must, however, accept those times and events that have created ballast in my life.

We all must move forward, no matter our history. Part of the equipment necessary to move forward is accepting who we are now, and we can't accept who we are if we don't accept those events that worked together to create who we are.

I remember heading towards the sacristy door one evening after mass when Fr. Schmid was closing the door from the inside. Papered window intact. He saw me coming but closed the door anyhow. There was no doubt another altar boy in there. I was sad. Did I want his attention? No, yes, no. Was I jealous that someone else was receiving his attentions? I believe I was. If there was a juvenile version of Stockholm syndrome, I was right in the middle of it.

The weight of my ballast has kept my ship afloat. Who would I have been without it? I don't know, and I don't have the time or energy to squander wondering about it. I have allowed the hate and hurt to become wrapped in compassion and empathy. People are fragile, and we all disembark the womb with a blank passport immediately stamped by external forces.

I have no way of knowing what Jimmy Schmid's life was as a child in 1940s Ireland. What events moulded him, directed him, influenced, and imprinted him. Who was he, who was it that hurt him? I am capable of compassion and humanity. There is simply always sadness in waste. A life he wasted was no doubt one that he did not live as he idealistically envisioned for himself.

The same applies to my mother. I did not walk in her shoes. She was raised during the great depression, with little education and an oppressive church influence. In her later years, her redemption was received as a grandmother. She was a much better gramma than she was a mother. I will never know whether it was simply the mellowing of age or an intentional effort towards absolution.

Chapter 16

STOCKHOLM AND MY OWN SKIN

Perhaps the greatest challenge of a lifetime such as mine is the constant struggle to fit within one's own skin. The world I grew up in did not have the "you be you" mindset that is refreshingly popular today.

My pre-pubescent forced coming of age had interrupted an immeasurable number of natural adolescent processes. Early life had diverted physical, psychological, sexual, and emotional paths of discovery to that isolated emotional crossroads where nefarious transactions and covenants occur.

My father was a minimal presence in my life, and he was eventually ostracized into oblivion through the resounding dominant influence of my mother. Personally, as a father, I would have fought more to remain a presence in my children's lives, but judging by his receding from my memories, or lack of memories, he did not.

In response to his lack of existence (which she had been dominant in accomplishing), my mother would send me to the church rectory to spend the evening and night with the priests. She insisted that I needed a male influence in my life. I did receive that in me.

Having no solid male influence in my home or life, and the only impact I had being an abusive one, I began to hate but crave the abuse. It represented what I determined to be my self-value. In a Stockholm way, I began to have an emotional, physical, and sexual response to my captor. Emotionally emaciated, I became drawn to the abuse as long as some form of sensitive acceptance accompanied it.

Sexual encounters were always a common factor that validated the male influence I craved. It imprinted on my soul, and it became a fundamental indulgence in the developing catechism of my spirituality. My altar-boy friends and I would experiment and engage in adolescent mutual masturbation in the already recognizable darker corners of the church. No doubt that we were all schooled at the literal feet of the same instructors. We were good friends, rode our bikes together, played at the park, went home when the streetlights came on. We would spend the nights at each other's houses, sleep in the same beds, and continue to experiment and elevate our experiences.

In grade 7, my mother opened the door and turned on the light, finding a friend and me in an unmistakable compromised encounter. She turned off the light and closed the door. Grade 7 was when I first seriously discovered my added attraction to females. At a neighbourhood pool party with classmates from school, I touched anatomy I had never felt before. It was monumental for me to learn that this facet of me also existed. It was significant enough that I still remember that "Precious and Few" by the appropriately named band Climax was playing on an LP.

In the end, as usual, life abandoned me to flesh out the internal workings of my young existence. Ideas, thoughts, fears, sexuality, social norms, religious rules, friendships were all deposited in me as seeds that germinated into the reasonably complex, empathetic, but tightly wound person I would eventually become. High school was horrific. How could I belong anywhere if I didn't even belong in my own skin? The only redeeming element of those days was the small, tightly knit, sexually charged and mostly formerly abused group that I stood and laid alongside. It was a sexual fellowship of the suffering which acted as an intimate balm applied to unattributable wounds.

In the liturgy of my soul, it is the apocryphal chapters that determine me. Tennessee Williams once said, "If you kill off all my demons, then my angels might also die." I get it and I have no choice but to agree. The universal truths of 'me,' however, remain. Where I seek affirmation, how I perceive self-value, the method I internalize love and affection, and who I see in the mirror are all imprinted and embedded within me.

I have journeyed through Catholicism, found discipline in independent Christianity, dabbled in the human truths of eastern mysticism, and embraced the understanding and maturity of reform Judaism. They also each define me.

My need to be right has also diminished, and I no longer attempt to engage in great philosophical or spiritual debates fueled by empty pint glasses on the bar top. Believe as you choose. You are on your journey, and I have no desire to measure or judge that journey by the yardstick of my own.

While I don't recommend the path I've travelled to anyone, I must embrace it. You can never move ahead if you don't accept where you are. And you can never accept where you are if you don't embrace the experiences which brought you here. Use them to develop strength. Use them to inspire empathy. Use them for the restoration of others.

A great prophet somewhere once said, "It's the hard cut and intricate pattern in the sole of your sandal that gives you the best stability and strongest grip; unfortunately, it also tends to hold onto the greatest amount of dog shit." I think that wisdom somehow applies.

Embrace the suck. You be you. I am finally reasonably comfortable in my own skin.

Chapter 17

THE PATH FORWARD AND A PERCEIVED END-STATE

I could continue to write and add chapters, but to what end?

Each new chapter would recall a specific time or experience in my life, ravaged by spectres from the past. But enough is enough. I could have been much more descriptive and graphic with each recollection of the abuse. But to what end? I attempted to present each event, as openly as possible, from my perspective within the time and space it occurred. I am confident that the reader understands the gravity of each situation and can fill in the blanks.

I could add more about my childhood's dysfunctional home life. The police at the door. The fights on the front lawn. The neighbours watching. I could talk about being woke up at 3 am and dragged outside, used as 'props for cops' to validate the abused wife scenario. Crying children always added credence, and fortunately for her, we were already crying. My home was broken. How much it was broken, how deeply the cracks in the foundation were exploited for the personal gratification of a debauched individual, I will never know.

My home life may have been responsible for a lot, but much of the state of my home life was also determined and intentionally degraded by those wearing clerical collars. Fr. Schmid betrayed his calling, victimized those he should have consoled, and as a spiritual carnivorous shepherd, he slaughtered and consumed his sheep. But and I say this with absolute literal sincerity, enough about him.

As a senior officer in the military, I repeatedly heard myself ask, "and what is the desired end-state?" It might be a great plan and have the best intentions, but what is the objective? What is the mission? What is ground zero, and by what events will you determine success? I ask myself the same as I draw close to completing my writings.

It is about me, but I don't want it to be about me. I want it to be about the other hundreds of thousands of me's out there. Has there been personal healing in the process of writing this? I don't know, and I genuinely don't at this point. I feel like the correct answer is yes, but right now, I've just pulled the scabs off, and the wounds are tender.

My perceived end-state is that it would in some way help someone whose young childhood was similar. I want them to know that their experience was not isolated. It is possible to walk through the sewer and yet be clean again. To succeed, prosper, be compassionate, accepting, and empathetic to those who are also struggling.

And to everyone else. Slow down, shut up, close your mouth, open your ears, open your eyes, open your hearts. Everyone is damaged, and everyone is hurting. Intentionally try to take moments during the day that are not about you.

I left my rank and such on my name as the author of this book. Not for any personal distinction or privilege, and anyone who knows me knows I'm not about that. But to demonstrate that you never know who is suffering or where they came from.

If this book creates even a small amount of healing for the wounded, visibility for the suffering, and understanding and compassion for the onlookers, then I guess I reached my end-state.

I leave you with,

The Prayer of Saint Francis

Lord, make me an instrument of your peace:
where there is hatred, let me sow love;
where there is injury, pardon;
where there is doubt, faith;
where there is despair, hope;
where there is darkness, light;
where there is sadness, joy.

O divine Master, grant that I may not so much seek
to be consoled as to console,
to be understood as to understand,
to be loved as to love.
For it is in giving that we receive,
it is in pardoning that we are pardoned,
and it is in dying that we are born to eternal life.

www.ingramcontent.com/pod-product-compliance
Lightning Source LLC
Chambersburg PA
CBHW070919080526
44589CB00013B/1363